DATE DUE			

Some Questions about Language

A Theory of Human Discourse and Its Objects

Some Questions about Language

Mortimer J. Adler

Open Court
La Salle, Illinois

Copyright © 1976 by Open Court Publishing Co.

All rights reserved. No part of this publication may be reproduced, stored in a retrieval system, or transmitted, in any form or by any means, electronic, mechanical, photocopying, recording, or otherwise, without the prior written permission of the publisher, Open Court Publishing Co., Box 599, La Salle, Illinois 61301. Printed in the United States of America.

Library of Congress Cataloging in Publication Data

Adler, Mortimer Jerome, 1902-
　　Some questions about language.

　　　1.　Languages—Philosophy.　2.　Languages—Psychology.
I.　Title.
P106.A3　　　　　　401　　　　　　75-1221
ISBN 0-87548-320-8

To Jacques Maritain

Analytical Table of Contents

Preface

$\mathcal{T}$he subject of this book has been of continuing interest to me over a span of fifty years. My first engagement with it occurred in 1922 when I delivered before the Graduate Philosophy Club of Columbia University a paper on the philosophy and psychology of meaning. Further, in my memory of stages in the development of my thought about the subject are lectures that I delivered at St. John's College in Annapolis in 1938; lectures delivered at the University of Chicago and at Yale University in the 1940s and 1950s; certain chapters and notes in *The Difference of Man and The Difference It Makes*, published in 1967; and once again lectures delivered at St. John's College in 1971 and 1972.

The most recent lectures at St. John's College are distinguished from all the earlier formulations in that they reflect sustained research and discussion of the subject carried on at the Institute for Philosophical

Research beginning in 1966. That work began to bear fruit in 1969, when John N. Deely joined the Institute's staff as a Senior Research Fellow and undertook to carry forward the researches and discussions that have eventuated in the writing of this book. Dr. Deely has surveyed the vast contemporary literature dealing with theories of language, some of them philosophical, some not. In addition, the discussions in which he and I have engaged have contributed to my understanding of certain points in traditional doctrines that bear on the problems of language, and sharpened my understanding of other points in ancient and mediaeval thought that help to solve those problems. I am indebted to him and regret that unresolved differences of opinion between us about certain aspects of a theory that we otherwise share prevent him from associating his name with mine in the authorship of this book. He will presently publish under his own name articles expressing his reservations or dissenting views; one such forthcoming article is cited in the Bibliographical Appendix.

I have long been of the opinion that the exposition of a philosophical doctrine should be as spare, trim, and structured as the demonstration of a sequence of theorems in a mathematical monograph. I know of no better way to achieve these qualities than by an orderly series of questions which pose the problems that a philosophical theory attempts to solve.

In every chapter or section of the exposition, the reader should be informed of the questions to be answered and told why they have been raised. Then, as he proceeds from question to question, he should be left in no doubt about the state of the argument and the direction of the analysis.

Too often a philosophical work compels the reader to peruse page after page of discussion before he finds out, if he ever does, what problem or problems the discussion hopes to resolve. Sometimes he is even compelled to formulate the problems for himself, inferring what they are from the general drift of the discussion.

This seems to me wasteful of the reader's energies and a source of distraction, if not bemusement, to his mind. It also permits the writer to digress—to follow many bypaths and plough through many thickets of questionable bearing. The relevance of the writer's remarks or observations, and even of his arguments, has not been rigorously controlled by a set of very specific questions that call for clear and satisfactory answers and for nothing beyond that.

I have tried to make the exposition of the philosophical doctrine that is the substance of this book meet the requirements just set forth. But in one respect the exposition must differ from the order of a mathematical treatise, in which the demonstration of an earlier theorem does not depend on the theorems or demonstrations that follow. A philosophical exposition cannot be that rigid in order. The reader of this book will find that, in some cases, the answer to an earlier question will explicitly mention but will also postpone for later treatment matters that affect the answer being given. Until later questions are answered, the earlier answers may not be fully understood, adequately supported, or cogently defended.

The manner of exposition that I have adopted precludes, as incongruous, the citation of particular authors, ancient or modern, whose theories are wholly rejected, criticized and corrected, or modified and amplified. It also precludes quotations from their writings, footnote commentaries on them, and polemical digressions in which ad hoc arguments are developed.

I have added two sections at the end of the book in the hope of compensating somewhat for these preclusions. One is an Epilogue which is partly historical and partly polemical in character and in which particular philosophers are mentioned by name. The other is a Bibliographical Appendix which is divided into four sections. The first lists writers with whose theories of language the theory expounded in this book is in most fundamental disagreement. The second lists writers whose theories are rejected on certain points but accepted on others. The third lists writers whose theories are accepted on essential points, but modified, amplified, or corrected on others. In addition, there is a fourth section that lists a number of other books or articles which have been examined but which are judged to be of minor relevance to the theory expounded in this book.

Readers of this book will come to it either well versed in or unacquainted with the literature on the philosophy of language, both traditional and contemporary. For those who are not acquainted with the literature, the absence of footnotes and of reference to particular authors will not be an impediment to their understanding of the theory here being proposed or of the views which it criticizes or rejects. However, if they become interested in controversial points, the Bibliographical Appendix will direct their attention to the works they should examine to pursue that interest.

For those who are well versed in the literature of the subject, footnotes and references to particular authors are not necessary. They will recognize the theories being criticized or rejected. However, even for them, the four-part Bibliographical Appendix may be useful as a guide to the main points at issue in the controversy on which this book takes a definite stand.

The dedication of this book, out of friendship and gratitude, to Jacques Maritain reflects not only a long personal association but also a particular debt. It was the reading of his *Degrees of Knowledge,* translated and published in 1938, which gave me the pivotal insight that is indispensable to a solution of the basic problem of meaning; and it was that book, as well as other writings of Maritain, especially his little essay "Sign and Symbol" (in *Ransoming the Time,* 1941), which brought to my attention the *Treatise on Signs* by Jean Poinsot. A translation by Dr. Deely of this portion of Poinsot's *Cursus Philosophicus,* done in the course of his work on language at the Institute for Philosophical Research, is scheduled for publication in the near future.

I wish, in addition, to express my gratitude to colleagues at the Institute who have read the manuscript of this book and given me the benefit of their criticisms and suggestions: Charles Van Doren, William Gorman, Otto Bird, John Van Doren, and William O'Meara. To the Aspen Institute for Humanistic Studies and to its President, Joseph Slater, I am indebted for providing the auspices, under which this book was written, as Scholar-in-residence at Aspen during the summer of 1973.

Mortimer J. Adler
Chicago
June, 1974

Some Questions about Language

A Theory of Human Discourse and Its Objects

One.
The Scope of a
Philosophy of Language

Preamble

$\mathcal{L}$anguage being the subject of
many inquiries, there are many approaches to the consideration of its
origin and nature, its properties and uses, its defects and the ways of
overcoming them. Philosophy is only one among the disciplines or
modes of inquiry that are concerned with language. This concern on
the part of philosophy may have arisen initially from difficulties encountered in the use of language for philosophical discourse; but it ex-
tends beyond that to the uses of language in ordinary discourse, in all
other disciplines, and for all other purposes; nor can philosophy avoid
being concerned with the substitution of specially constructed
languages for ordinary language as instruments of discourse.

While the philosophical interest in language would thus appear to
be all-encompassing in scope, the philosophical approach to language is
in fact limited to the kind of questions that it is legitimate for a

3

philosopher to try to answer. There are many questions about language that can be answered only by historical research, by the empirical methods of the social and behavioral sciences, or by one or another field of humanistic scholarship, such as philology. It is necessary, therefore, to define the scope of a philosophy of language by stating the problems with which philosophy is competent to deal, and by drawing a line of demarcation that separates these problems from other closely related problems that are beyond philosophy's scope and, in addition, are posterior; that is, cannot be adequately dealt with unless and until prior problems have been solved.

This book as a whole is an effort to formulate the basic philosophical problems about language and to propose solutions to them. In this opening chapter, I can do no more than indicate the direction that will be taken in the chapters to follow. I will do this by trying to answer the following questions: 1. What is the primary fact that a philosophy of language should try to explain or account for? 2. What aspects of language should a philosophical approach to the subject not attempt to deal with? 3. What, specifically, should be avoided in developing a philosophical theory of language? 4. How are the philosophical problems of language related to the concerns of the logician and the grammarian in dealing with language?

Question 1. What is the primary fact that a philosophy of language should try to explain or account for?

It is either a fact or an illusion that men, using language, are able to converse or discourse with one another about matters that are public, not private. A private matter is something that is accessible to one person and one person alone, and so, strictly speaking, cannot be the subject of discourse or conversation involving two or more individuals addressing themselves to that item of consideration, whatever it is. All other matters are public, or are capable of being so. (I shall elaborate on this distinction between public and private in Chapter IV, Questions 6 and 7.)

That public matters are largely the topics of conversation among men is generally regarded as a fact beyond dispute. Yet, on the one hand, men do appear sometimes to talk to one another about a matter that is private to one of them; and, on the other hand, when they do talk to one another about a matter that they regard as something to which they have equal access, they may be deceived by their use of language into thinking that this is so; in fact, they may have nothing in common to talk about.

I propose to regard conversation about public matters as a fact even when it is clear that the items being discussed do not exist in the physical world. That men are able to talk to one another about the physical furniture in a room that they are occupying would seem to be beyond question. They certainly also appear able to talk to one another about many items that are not present to their senses in the way that the furniture is—past events that they remember, future contingencies that they imagine or conjecture, and even items the existence of which, past, present, or future, they question and the actual or possible reality of which they discuss with one another.

It is my contention that the experience of communicating with one another, which men have when they talk to one another about items that are not immediately present to their senses, is not just an illusion to be explained away, but a reality to be explained. Only if what is here asserted to be a reality cannot be satisfactorily explained does it become a questionable assumption or even an illusion that needs to be exposed for what it is. The task of a philosophy of language, as I see it, is to construct a theory that attempts to explain the reality or fact of communication which I have taken as its point of departure. Only if we fail in that task are we required to reexamine that point of departure and ask ourselves whether what we, and men generally, take to be a reality or a fact is, after all, only an illusion or an appearance concerning which we have all been long deceived.

In thus defining the task of a philosophy of language, I am stating its minimal obligation. There are undoubtedly other things that a philosophical theory of language should do, but this is the least it can do; and if it does not discharge this first and minimal obligation, it is not in a position to do anything else well. The philosophical questions about language with which this book will be concerned all fall within the ambit of this primary task. To answer those questions, the theory that is advanced and defended will be a minimal theory, dealing not with all, but only with some of the questions about language that are proper for philosophers to consider.

Question 2. What aspects of language should a philosophical approach to the subject not attempt to deal with?

The use of language to express the emotions, wishes, desires, or decisions of the speaker, to convey his requests or commands to others, or to announce or recommend courses of action, is probably as frequent and commonplace as the use of language for the purpose of making statements about what is or is not the case, may or may not be the case, must or cannot be the case. Statements of the latter sort must be either true or false, whereas utterances of the former sort may be neither; when they are true, they are so only because the speaker intends to tell the truth, and when false, they are so only because the speaker indulges in intentional prevarication.

What is common to these two uses is that both may involve communication, though they need not. Insofar as any use of language involves communication, it necessarily involves the problem of how two or more individuals have some matter or item commonly before them to which they are giving their attention, or some aspect of which they are considering in one way or another. To the extent that it involves communication, and only to that extent, does the use of language fall within the scope of a philosophical theory that attempts to discharge the primary task defined in the answer to Question 1. This stricture imposes two limitations on the theory to be developed.

The first and most important of these is the elimination of any concern with the truth or falsity of the statements that men make about reality. False statements are as readily communicable as true ones. The problem of what is involved in their being means of communication is antecedent to and independent of the problem of what is involved in their being true or false. Nevertheless, a philosophical theory of language should be able to explain how men who are engaged in talking about some common matter or item can agree or disagree about the truth or falsity of what is being said. It should be concerned with how

6

statements can be clear and precise enough to be judged either true or false. The philosophy of language is obliged to show that such judgments are at least possible; but it is obliged to go no further than that. It stops short of the logical problems involved in showing how sentences must be interpreted in order to construe out of them propositions that are clear and precise enough to be judged true or false.

There are a number of different logical theories or systems which address themselves to this problem and offer different solutions of it. None is a theory of language as such; all presuppose a philosophy of language, sometimes explicitly, sometimes surreptitiously. A philosophical theory of language, particularly one that discharges the primary task of explaining communication among men in their discourse about public matters (i.e., items that are commonly accessible to their consideration), is antecedent to any logical theory that is concerned with construing statements so that they can be judged either true or false. A philosophy of language, in short, is concerned with the communicability of statements that can be either true or false, but not with their truth or falsity.

The second limitation, like the first, excludes from the consideration of a philosophy of language those aspects of emotive or illocutionary utterances which go beyond their being instruments of communication. Insofar as such utterances may be about private rather than public matters, such as an individual's feelings or desires, they do raise a problem for the philosopher of language, for then it becomes necessary to explain how two individuals can talk to one another about something that, at first glance, appears to be exclusively private—a feeling experienced by one of them and not by the other. How utterances that express feelings or convey commands can be intended as communications and can be received as such is a problem that does belong to the philosophy of language; but here, as in the case of statements that can be true or false, there are logical problems about the various ways in which such utterances can be construed that are not the concern of a philosophy of language and are consequent or dependent upon the solution of the antecedent problems with which the philosophy of language is properly concerned.

Question 3. What, specifically, should be avoided in developing a philosophical theory of language?

In order to explain the fact which is its point of departure—the fact that men converse with one another about matters or items that are commonly accessible to their consideration—a philosophical theory of language cannot avoid making certain commitments that involve assertions about the existence of things other than language itself. This amounts to no more than saying that a theory which aims to explain something is required to posit whatever is needed to account for that which it sets out to explain. For example, it may be necessary to posit the existence of something as unobservable as the human mind in order to explain how language serves the purposes of communication; it may, further, be necessary to posit certain things about the way in which the mind works.

The only justification to be given for such posits is that they are indispensable to the explanation of the facts to be accounted for. In this respect, a philosophy of language does not differ from a theory about anything else, whether it be scientific or philosophical. Any theory that seeks to explain facts or phenomena may be obliged to posit unobservable entities or operations, sometimes called "theoretical constructs," in order to discharge its function of accounting for that which is to be explained; and the only justification it can ever give, or ever needs to give, for such posits is that they are indispensable to the explanation that is called for.

I have so far mentioned the philosophical commitments that may not be avoidable in developing a theory of language which undertakes to explain the phenomena of human discourse as involving communication among men. All of these, as indicated above, should be posits consequent upon the effort to explain the chosen phenomena. None should be prior to it. That is what should be avoided in developing a philosophical theory of language; namely, philosophical commitments about the shape of the world, the structure of reality, the character of its constituents, or their relationships.

Most specifically, a philosophical theory of language should avoid prior commitments about what really does exist and can exist or about what does not exist in reality and cannot; commitments about what is knowable or unknowable; and commitments about the relation that obtains between the human mind and the human body, if they are distinct in any sense whatsoever. In other words, a philosophy of language should avoid ontological, epistemological, and psychological commitments that are in any way prior to the consideration of the phenomena of language it seeks to explain. The philosopher of language should come to that effort with complete neutrality toward all the ontological, epistemological, or psychological commitments of which he may be aware. He may in the end turn out to favor some of these as opposed to others, but if he does, he must do so only as a consequence of his effort to explain the phenomena under consideration. The commitments he makes must be posterior, not prior, commitments—posits made solely for the explanatory purpose at hand.

The reason for this controlling stricture on the theory to be developed is not difficult to state. A philosophy of language that involved prior philosophical commitments would necessarily beg questions of truth and falsity that are not its function to decide. Such prior commitments may inevitably lead to espousing the view that ordinary language does not serve the purpose of stating the truth about reality and that, for the said purpose, a special language needs to be logically constructed. It would adopt this course because of its prior commitment to one among several competing views of reality and also because it held the view that a philosophically satisfactory language must perfectly mirror the "realities" to which it was committed. Such a theory of language, philosophically preconditioned, would thus beg all the questions that philosophers in disagreement with one another must employ language to discuss. Only by avoiding prior ontological, epistemological, and psychological commitments, can a theory of language leave such questions open and allow philosophers in disagreement about them to use language without any prejudgment of the issues to be discussed or disputed.

As will become manifest in what follows, there are grounds for thinking that ordinary language not only serves the purposes of communication among men in discourse about the commonplace matters of daily life, but that it also can serve the purposes of philosophers engaged in discourse about the issues that concern them. If it has defects and difficulties as a means of communication, as it most certainly does, these can be remedied or overcome by devices that correct its misuses and perfect its use. We need not abandon it and replace it with a system of logical constructions that draw their inspiration from question-begging commitments to certain, very special philosophical views about the constituents and structure of reality.

When we go beyond the use of language for the purposes of discourse about the affairs of daily life, we perceive that it may have to be enriched by the addition of words that belong to one or another technical vocabulary in order to serve the special purposes of philosophical, scientific, or scholarly discourse. It may even have to be largely transformed by the introduction of special symbols, as in the case of mathematics. Nevertheless, if a theory of language succeeds in explaining how language serves the purpose of communication about the affairs of daily life, then it will apply not only to ordinary language used for that purpose but also to ordinary language enriched or altered for the purposes of philosophical, scientific, and mathematical discourse.

Question 4. How are the philosophical problems of language related to the concerns of the logician and the grammarian in dealing with language?

The answer to the preceding question determines the general tenor of the answer to this one. As the logician is ultimately concerned with the capacity of statements to be true or false, and with the rules governing the validity or invalidity of statements in relation to one another, so the grammarian is concerned with correctness and incorrectness in the syntax of speech, and with the rules governing the ways in which words should or should not be related. Though they may not be exclusively normative, the disciplines of logic and grammar are certainly regulative in application. Even apart from their regulative function, logic and grammar, as sciences, presuppose the existence of language as an instrument of communication. Their problems are, therefore, posterior to the philosophical concern with the phenomena of communication.

I. Scope of a Philosophy of Language

Not only is a philosophy of language prior to logic and grammar; it must also be formulated so as to be completely neutral with respect to the plurality of logics and the variety of theoretical grammars or systems of linguistics. Its formulations should be unaffected by the preference for one system of logic as against another, or the preference for one theoretical grammar or linguistic system as against another. What has just been said would still hold true even if there were a universal grammar, or a single all-encompassing logic that provided a transformation formula for diverse systems of logic.

Two.
The Primary Problem for a Philosophy of Language

There is one property of language about which universal agreement exists. Whatever else can be said about language, one indisputable fact about it is that its component elements—its words and sentences—possess a property that has been variously called "sense," "significance," or "meaning." Meaningless marks or sounds, however they may be arranged or used, do not constitute a language. A meaningless language is a contradiction in terms. A foreign language that an individual does not understand may be meaningless to him, but he recognizes that it is a language, nevertheless, when he realizes that it is meaningful to someone else and that, by an effort on his part, it can become meaningful to him.

There is, in addition, one other fact about language that has never been disputed; namely, that its constituent physical elements—its sounds and marks—are initially meaningless entities. In and of

13

themselves they do not, by their very natures, possess the property of meaning. Somehow they acquire that property by human intervention. Just how they do so is one of the problems to be solved; and as will become clear, that problem, though concerned with the genesis of meaning in the transformation of meaningless sounds or marks into meaningful words, is philosophical rather than historical or psychological. It is concerned with the factors that must be operative for any mark or sound to become a meaningful word in any language, not with how a particular word acquired its meaning in the development of a particular language, or with the learning process in which some mark or sound became meaningful for this individual or that.

I shall use the word "notation" to cover the physical marks, sounds, or bodily gestures that are initially meaningless and become words, usually with multiple meanings registered in the lexicon of a language. The physical properties of such notations remain exactly the same when they are meaningless and when they are meaningful. The sounds of Russian, for example, are exactly the same audible sounds for a person who understands Russian and for one who does not. For the person who understands Russian, those sounds are meaningful sounds constituting words and sentences; whereas for the person who does not understand Russian, they are merely perceptible physical events, having the same audible qualities, but meaningless.

A meaningless word is as much a contradiction in terms as a meaningless language. If a physical notation is totally without meaning, it will not be found in the dictionary of any language, and so it will not be a word. Nonsense syllables are not listed in any lexicon. They represent notations which may become words, but so long as they remain nonsense syllables they are not words.

The two primary problems to be solved by a philosophy of language are, first, the one already indicated—the problem of the genesis of meaning or, what is the same, the problem of the factors involved in the transformation of meaningless notations into meaningful words; and second, the problem of what is meant by any meaningful word. Again it must be said that this is a philosophical, not an historical or a psychological, problem; it is not concerned with what is meant by a particular word in a particular language at a particular time, or as used by this individual or that at one time or another.

II. The Primary Problem

The two problems just stated are so related that they should not be enumerated as "first" and "second." They are really coordinate aspects of one basic problem—the problem of meaning. That is the basic problem in the philosophy of language precisely because, as I pointed out in the answer to Question 1 of Chapter I, the first and minimal obligation of a philosophy of language is to explain or account for language as an instrument of communication, through the use of which we are able to converse with one another about matters or items that we are able to consider in common. If the words of a language were not meaningful, communication would not take place. The utterance of a string of nonsense syllables by one person and audited by another does not engage them in discourse with one another.

Since the presence of meaning is indispensable to the communicative function of language, the explanation of meaning is indispensable to the explanation of language as an instrument of communication. Not any explanation of meaning will do, but only one that, in the way it accounts for the genesis and location of meaning, shows that what men appear to be doing when they engage in discourse and talk about items or matters that they are able to consider in common, is not an illusory appearance but a reality. Solutions of the problem of meaning that either deny or obscure this reality, or fail to account for it, must be rejected by a philosophy of language that takes its point of departure from, and finds its primary task in, the fact of communication.

In this chapter, I will try to answer the following questions: 1. Can the problem of meaning be formulated in a way that is not prejudicial to any possible solution of it? 2. What different meanings of the word "meaning" must be noted to achieve a clearer statement of the problem of meaning? 3. What mode of meaning is peculiar to words and what mode of meaning do words share with other things? 4. Is there only one mode of meaning peculiar to words, or are there two? 5. Can ambiguities latent in the word "meaning" be avoided? 6. Does the eulogistic use of the word "meaningful" and the dylogistic use of the word "meaningless" raise a problem for the philosophy of language? 7. Of the several modes of meaning (i.e., of signifying) that we have so far considered, and of the various uses of the word "meaning" that we have so far indicated, which concern the philosophy of language in dealing with its primary problem?

Answers to the foregoing questions should yield an unambiguous vocabulary for the clearest possible statement of the problem of meaning—the primary problem for a philosophy of language.

Question 1. Can the problem of meaning be formulated in a way that is not prejudicial to any possible solution of it?

It would appear to be possible to formulate the problem of meaning in such a way that no solution of it is favored and none is excluded. This can be done by identifying meaning as that which constitutes the *difference* between a physical event or entity (i.e., a sound or a mark) as a part of nature or even as a part of human experience and that same physical event or entity as a part of speech—an element of language. Meaning is that which makes the difference between a mere notation (i.e., a sound or mark) and a word (i.e., a part of speech); and this difference can be recognized and is generally acknowledged by those who advance competing theories of how a notation becomes a word or who hold conflicting views of the property possessed by words and not by notations.

What has just been neutrally identified as the meaning to be accounted for may not be the only mode of meaning, or meaning in every sense of that term, but it is at least linguistic meaning—the meaning that is a property of the words of a language, including all the words that a comprehensive lexicon sets forth and all the meanings it assigns to those words. It is what makes a word a word instead of a mere physical notation—an audible sound or a visible mark. It is what makes a sentence a sentence instead of nothing but a sequence of marks or sounds.

While it is true that an individual may realize that the marks on the page of a Russian book are words and sentences in that language, they are not, strictly speaking, words and sentences for him so long as he understands no Russian. The question of how those meaningless marks become meaningful is exactly the same for the Russian child learning to read his native language and for the foreigner trying to learn Russian. Admittedly, the process of learning, viewed psychologically or

16

behaviorally, is not the same for both. The Russian child starts to learn his first language, whereas the foreigner starts with a language already acquired and then acquires a second one. But this difference does not affect the question with which the philosophy of language is concerned—the question concerning the factors that must be involved in any and every transformation of meaningless notations into meaningful words. What is required in order to endow them with meaning or to confer meaning upon them?

To deny the legitimacy of this question is to suppose that meaning occurs by spontaneous generation: that without the operation of any assignable causes or without the intervention of any extrinsic factors, the physical sound or mark suddenly becomes a word What at one moment is a meaningless notation becomes at the next a meaningful notation—a word or part of speech—without sufficient reason for the change. If this occurred, the genesis of meaning would be as mysterious and inexplicable as the genesis of life according to theories that affirm the spontaneous generation of living from nonliving matter.

Dismissing so outrageous a supposition, we are left with the question stated above: What causes or factors are operative in conferring meaning on physical notations and thus transforming them into words? To be sure that this question is understood, we must eliminate one response to it that clearly will not suffice. It will not do to say that what gives meaning to a meaningless notation, thus transforming it into a word, is the meaning already possessed by one or more other notations that are meaningful, i.e., sounds or marks that are already words.

This does happen, of course, when we are confronted with a strange "word"—to speak exactly, a notation that we recognize is potentially a word and will become actually a word for us when we discover its meaning. The individual who, confronted with a notation that he recognizes to be an English word, but the meaning of which he does not know, says of it that "it is just Greek to me," is acknowledging that that English word is still just a mere notation for him but that, at the same time, the notation in question is a word for other English-speaking individuals.

In this situation, the individual may have recourse to a dictionary to learn the meaning or meanings of the notation that was, at first glance, a strange "word" or just a notation for him and so not yet a word he can use. But this procedure, while adequate for some notations, is not and cannot be adequate for all. If an individual's only approach to or means of learning a foreign language were a dictionary of that language, and one which used that language exclusively, he could not learn the meaning of any of its words. Only on the condition that he already knows or can somehow learn the meaning of a certain number of words without the use of a dictionary, can a dictionary become useful as a way of learning the meaning of still other words in the language.

The relationship of the words in a dictionary is a completely closed circle, in which each word has a meaning that is stated in terms of other words. This enables us to learn the meaning of the strange "words" in the language represented by the dictionary, but it does not enable us to explain how any of the words that the dictionary contains acquired the various lexically enumerated meanings that each of them has. For a child to get to the point at which he can move effectively within the circle of a dictionary, some meaningless notations must first have become meaningful words for him—and become so without the help of a dictionary. The dictionary, therefore, cannot be the answer to the philosophical question (I repeat, philosophical, *not* historical or psychological, question) of how meaningless marks or sounds become meaningful words, the question concerning the causes or factors that must be operative to account for this transformation.

Question 2. What different meanings of the word "meaning" must be noted to achieve a clearer statement of the problem of meaning?

Almost all the words in the dictionary of any language have more than one meaning attached to them. The word "meaning" is no exception. However, it is not necessary for our purposes to examine a complete inventory of the meanings of the word "meaning" and such associated words as "means" and "meant"; nor need we consider all the different ways in which these words are and can be used in ordinary speech. In this and in the following questions, I will restrict myself to noting only those distinctions which are indispensable to the clarification of the philosophical problem with which we are concerned. To begin with, let us consider the distinction between the use of the word "meaning" as a verb and as a noun.

We use the word "meaning" as a verb when we speak of the action of pointing to, standing for, or referring. We say that one item (whatever it is) *means* another (whatever it is). "Meaning" is a participle of the verb "to mean." Let X symbolize the first item mentioned above, and Y the second. In the formula "X means Y," both of the items, X and Y, may be words, X may be a word and Y something other than a word, or both may be nonverbal entities. The relationship between X and Y will be different when X and Y differ in the ways indicated above. I will deal with one of these differences in Question 3 to follow. Here I wish only to observe that the action of meaning involves a relationship between something that means and something that is meant.

When we speak of that which is meant, we are using the word "meaning" as a noun. In the formulation "X means Y," we speak of the second term in the relationship as the meaning of the first. When we say that the word "X" has several distinct meanings, we are saying that "X" not only means Y, but also Z and W and that in their relationship to "X" as that which means them, Y, Z, and W are the meanings of "X"—the several distinct items which are meant. I have used symbols to represent this relationship in order to avoid begging any questions about the character of that which is meant, especially when Y, Z, and W each stand for something that is not a word.

One further point should be observed here, even though its full significance will not become manifest until later. We speak of a notation as acquiring a meaning or of a word as changing its meaning—gaining one meaning, perhaps, and losing another. Such speech calls attention to the fact that the notation, before it becomes a word, does not have a meaning; and to the fact that notations are words only when they do have meaning. In terms of the distinction between the verb-use and the noun-use of the word "meaning," the having of meaning by a word involves both (i) its standing in a certain relationship to something else, and also (ii) the something else which is the term of that relationship. When the word "X" has the meaning Y, (i) it *means* Y, and (ii) it has Y as its meaning.

Can we ever say that something is, rather than has, a meaning? We appear to do so when, using the word "meaning" as a noun, we say that Y *is* the meaning of the word "X," or is one of the meanings that the word "X" *has*. When, using the word "meaning" as a verb, we say that X means Y, without specifying whether X stands for a word or for something other than a word, an interesting series of questions arises. Does X acquire the relationship to Y that is involved in X's meaning Y? Is that relationship something which X has or may not have, because it may or may not acquire it, or having it, may lose it? Or, in sharp contradistinction, is X such that, by virtue of what it is, it is always in a certain relationship to Y; and being in that relationship rather than having it, it can neither acquire nor lose it?

I will return to these questions in Chapter III. For the present, suffice it to observe that the distinction between the verb-use and the noun-use of the word "meaning" enables us to achieve a clearer statement of the two related aspects of the problem of meaning. The two aspects of the problem can be stated in the form of two related questions: (i) How does a notation which initially lacks meaning later come to mean this or that, and thereby become transformed into a word? (ii) What is meant by the meaningful word which the notation has become? The aspect of the problem which is concerned with the acquirement of meaning by a meaningless notation can be further defined by recognizing that what the notation has acquired, in acquiring meaning, is a relationship to something else. The second aspect of the problem also becomes clear when we recognize that what we are asking about is that something else—the other term in the relationship, namely, that which is meant.

Question 3. What mode of meaning is peculiar to words and what mode of meaning do words share with other things?

We have seen that meaning involves a relationship between X and Y when X means Y. We have also noted that this relationship may occur between X and Y under three conditions: (i) when X and Y are both words; (ii) when X is a word and Y is something other than a word; and (iii) when neither X nor Y are words. This enumeration appears to be exhaustive. A fourth alternative can be stated, in which X is something other than a word and Y is a word, but that logical possibility appears to be null and void. Something other than a word (or other than a symbol of some kind which functions as a word functions) never means a word.

The two modes of meaning that we are here concerned to distinguish involve (*a*) the relationship of meaning that obtains between X and Y when X is a word and Y is something other than a word, and (*b*) the relationship of meaning that obtains between X and Y when neither X nor Y are words. The relationship of meaning that obtains when X and Y are both words is one that is peculiar to words and to nothing else. But may it not be the case that the kind of relationship which X has to Y when X is a word and Y is something other than a word can also obtain when neither of the two entities is a word? And, similarly, must we not ask whether the kind of relationship which X has to Y when neither X nor Y are words can also obtain when X is a word and Y is something other than a word? These are the questions I will now try to answer.

Let me begin with the relationship of meaning that obtains between two entities neither of which is a word. We say that clouds mean rain, that smoke means fire, that the sound of the dinner-bell means that dinner is ready. Now let us contrast that relationship with the relationship of meaning that obtains between a word and something other than a word. We say that the word "rain" means rain, that the word "fire" means fire, and that the word "dinner" means dinner. On the face of it, the two relationships are so utterly different that it is difficult to see how they could ever be confused or go undistinguished. Yet among those who have tried to explain how meaningless notations acquire meaning and thus become meaningful words, some have advanced explanations that fail to distinguish between these two modes of meaning.

The distinction in question can most easily be made manifest by substituting other words for the word "meaning" in such statements as (1) "clouds mean rain" and (2) "the word 'rain' means rain." In the first case, we can say "clouds suggest or portend rain"; we might even say "clouds probably imply rain," using the word "imply" to stand for the "if-then" relationship which obtains between clouds and rain: if there are clouds of a certain sort in the sky, then it will probably rain. In the second case, we can say "the word 'rain' is the name of rain; it designates the phenomenon of rain, or refers to it." Here the relationship is one of naming, designating, or referring, not one of suggesting, portending, or implying. We cannot say "If the word 'rain' is used, then it will probably rain." Nor, on the other hand, can we say that clouds name, designate, or refer to rain. So far, then, it would appear to be the case that the mode of meaning which involves naming and is designative or referential involves a relationship that obtains only between a word and something other than a word; and it would also appear to be the case that the mode of meaning which involves the if-then relationship obtains only between entities neither of which is a word.

What appears to be the case with regard to the mode of meaning which involves naming, designation, or reference is in fact the case. It obtains only between a word and something other than a word, except for the special case in which a word refers to itself (see Chapter VII, Question 3). This is a mode of meaning that belongs to words alone. But the mode of meaning which involves the if-then relationship does not exclusively belong to entities which are not words. Thus, for example, we can use the word "dinner," spoken in the tone of an announcement, just as we can ring the dinner-bell, to announce the readiness of the meal. The same holds for the word "fire" and the ringing of the fire-bell; and for countless other words that function in this way by informing those who hear them that, if they are spoken in a certain tone of voice, the event they refer to is either about to occur or is occurring.

Let us now fortify this distinction by adopting the following vocabulary. Both the clouds that mean rain and the word "rain" that means rain can be called *signs* in a generic sense of the term *sign*, for each functions to bring to our attention something other than itself. But since they do not function as signs in the same way, let us call the kind of sign that signifies by suggesting, portending, or implying a *signal;* and let us call the kind of sign that signifies by naming, designating, or referring a *designator.* (I propose these terms for adoption rather than others that might serve the same purpose, because both *signal* and *designator* contain the root sign, and this should enable us to remember that they are both kinds or species of *sign.*)

It was pointed out above that while only a word like "fire" can be the designative-sign of fire, that same word can also be the signal-sign of fire, in the same way that smoke is the signal-sign of fire, or that the ringing of a fire-bell is. It was also pointed out that when we use the word "fire" as a signal, it functions in the same way that the ringing of the fire-bell does, to inform hearers that the event the word refers to is either about to occur or is occurring. It should be noted at once that while the ringing of the fire-bell functions as a signal without having any designative significance, since that ringing sound is certainly not the name of fire, the word "fire" functions as a signal only consequent upon its having designative significance as the name of fire. Just as the word "fire" cannot function as a signal that can be substituted for the ringing of a fire-bell unless it, first of all, functions as a name designating fire, so also the words uttered by a patient, which the psychoanalyst interprets as signals—or symptoms—of the patient's psychological condition, must first of all be understood by him in their meaning as designators. His interpretation of them as signals is consequent upon his understanding of them as designators.

This can be summed up by saying, first, that words alone are signs having designative significance; second, that both words and nonwords can be signs having signal significance; third, that when words, unlike nonwords, function as signs having signal significance, they do so only in consequence of their also being signs having designative significance; and hence, fourth, that it is their meaning as designators which is the primary significance of words as signs, not their meaning as signals.

The importance of this distinction between signs that are signals and signs that are designators, together with the fact that only words are designators (though they may also be, secondarily, signals), lies in its bearing on the problem of how anything that has meaning acquires its meaning. The clouds that signal rain and the smoke that signals fire are not man-made entities or events; whereas the word "fire" that designates fire and sometimes signals it is a man-made notation that has become a meaningful word; so, too, the ringing of the fire-bell that signals fire is a man-made instrumentality. The relationship between clouds and rain, or between smoke and fire, is a natural relationship and one that is observable by anyone attentive to the relevant phenomena. It is a relationship that certainly involves an often repeated temporal sequence between the observed phenomena, and may be thought to involve a causal relationship, clouds being the cause of rain, smoke the effect of fire. The ringing of the fire-bell is not a natural event, but a conventional device that men have resorted to for the purpose of signalling; and it, therefore, does not acquire its significance as a signal in the same way that clouds or smoke acquire their signal significance. The event being signalled (the fire) is neither cause nor effect of the fire-bell; nor need there be any temporal sequence or conjunction of fire-bell and fire to confer signal significance on the fire-bell.

In Chapter III, where I will attempt to solve the problem of how meaningful notations acquire meaning and become meaningful words, I will not only deal with the primary designative significance of words, but also with their secondary signal significance; and in that latter connection, I will try to explain how signal significance is acquired in somewhat different ways by (i) non-words that are natural entities or phenomena (such as smoke signalling fire), (ii) by non-words that are humanly contrived instrumentalities (such as the fire-bell signalling fire), and (iii) by words which have designative significance (such as the word "fire" signalling fire).

Question 4. Is there only one mode of meaning peculiar to words, or are there two?

We have seen that words alone function as names and have the mode of meaning that we have termed designative significance. The question now to be answered is whether all words have that mode of meaning, or only some words; and if the latter is the case, as I affirm

24

it to be, then I must ask, further, about the character of this other mode of meaning that words and words alone can have.

The answer that I have just affirmed, which is that some words have a mode of meaning that is *not* designative significance, amounts to saying that some words do not name anything or are not name-words; and that, not having designative significance, they do not refer to anything. Yet, being meaningful words, listed in a dictionary of the language and having therein one or more meanings attached to them, can it be the case that they mean without meaning anything; that is, without there being anything that is meant by them? Can there be a mode of meaning which does not involve a relationship between a sign (that which means) and a significate (that which is meant)?

This question has been a source of embarrassment from the very beginning to all who have philosophized about language and have tried to solve the basic problem of the meaning of words, in both aspects of that problem. It led the ancients to distinguish between two kinds of words which they called *categorematic* and *syncategorematic,* the former being all the name-words (but not necessarily only nouns) which have designative significance apart from the way in which they are used in sentences or in combination with other words; the latter being all the other words in the dictionary of the language, words which have significance only in terms of the ways in which they can be used in sentences or in combination with other words. This distinction, first introduced in antiquity, was elaborated in the Middle Ages, and has been employed or resorted to in various ways in modern times and in recent discussions of language.

Whatever else is involved in the distinction, one point appears to be clear. The words classified as categorematic have lexical meaning in their own right and without serving to qualify or modify the meaning possessed by other words. In contrast, the words classified as syncategorematic, and sometimes called "particles" (i.e., articles, such as "a" and "the"; prepositions, such as "of," "to," "by," "in"; conjunctions, such as "both/and"; disjunctions, such as "either/or," "not/both"; and such words as "is" or "is not" when they function solely as affirmative or negative copulas) do not have lexical meaning in their own right, but only when they serve to qualify, modify, or relate other words in significant phrases or sentences. The total significance of such phrases or sentences is not wholly given by the designative meaning of the categorematic words which they contain; it is always dependent on the meaning of the syncategorematic words which enter into combination with the categorematic words to constitute the significance of the phrase or sentence.

It is not my purpose here to give an exhaustive enumeration of syncategorematic words or to divide them into subgroups according to the different ways in which such words function syncategorematically. Clearly, they are not all of the same type, nor do they all function in the same way, as is evident from consideration of the difference between the syntactical role played by such words as "a" and "the," such words as "and" and "or," such words as the affirmative and negative copulas "is" and "is not." Suffice it here to note that, underlying these differences, what is common to all of them is the syntactical role they play in the construction of significant phrases and sentences. Though categorematic words also play a syntactical role in the construction of significant phrases and sentences, they have a lexical significance independent of their syntactical function. These facts help us to offer a preliminary answer to the question about the mode of meaning possessed by words that are not name-words and do not have designative significance.

To say that a word is not a name-word and does not have designative significance is tantamount to saying that it has no lexical significance apart from the syntactical role it plays in significant phrases or sentences. To go from that to saying that the word which is not a name-word has only syntactical significance merely reiterates that its meaning or significance consists in the ways in which it can be used to qualify, modify, or relate words that have designative significance. Another way of making the same point would be to say that the syntactical significance of syncategorematic words derives from the grammatical, rhetorical, or logical operations we use them to perform; in which case, we can equate their syntactical with their operative significance, and we can speak of syncategorematic words, which have such significance, as linguistic operators. All the words listed in the dictionary of a language can be exhaustively divided into name-words having designative significance and linguistic operators having syntactical significance.

This is, at most, a preliminary answer to the question posed. It definitely asserts that there is more than one mode of meaning which words and words alone can have; and, in addition, it asserts, that there are no more than two such modes—the designative significance of name-words and the syntactical significance of linguistic operators. But while thus answering the question posed, it fails to answer the further question that was raised about the mode of meaning possessed by linguistic operators, i.e., the question about that which is meant by them. It is acknowledged that, not having designative significance, they do not name or refer to anything, and yet, as we have conceded, they must have some sort of significate; for a meaningful word that is a sign cannot be totally without a significate, if meaning is a relation between that which means and that which is meant.

This problem cannot be solved until we have first solved the problem of how the primary words of a language—the categorematic or name-words—acquire the designative significance they possess; and also the problem of what it is they refer to—the character of that which is meant by them. This I hope to do in Chapter III, at which place I will return to question that remains to be answered concerning syncategorematic words or linguistic operators (see Chapter III, Question 6).

Question 5. Can ambiguities latent in the word "meaning" be avoided?

In the answers to the preceding questions, a vocabulary has emerged that should enable us to avoid ambiguities latent in the word "meaning."

To replace the word "meaning" used as a verb, as in the statement "X means Y," we can substitute the generic word "signifies"; and when we wish to be more specific about the way in which X signifies Y, we can use "signals," on the one hand, or "designates," "names," or "refers to," on the other.

As I have already indicated, the word "sign," like the word

"signifies," is generic, and it can be modified to indicate different types of signs: signal signs and designative signs, both of which are signifiers.

To replace the word "meaning" used as a noun to signify *that which is meant*, we can employ still another derivative from and associate of "sign" and "signifies," namely, "significate." When we say "X signifies Y," we can call X the sign or signifier and Y the significate of X. Instead of saying "X signifies Y" when the mode of significance of X is designative significance, we can say "X refers to Y," and we can call Y the referent of X. If X happens to be something like the smoke that signals fire, or the fire-bell that signals it, we would not call fire its referent; for we would only use that term when the mode of signifying is designative or referential, not when it is signalling. And just as "signifying" names the generic relation between X and Y when X signifies Y, so "signalling" and "reference" or "referring" name the two main modes of signifying that we have so far distinguished. The words "referring," "designating," and "naming" can be used interchangeably.

In addition, there is another pair of words that we can substitute for the word "meaning" used one time as a verb and another time as a noun, which is the ambiguous usage that we are seeking to eliminate or safeguard ourselves against. Just as we can use the word "signifies" for the act of meaning and the word "significate" for that which is meant, so we can use "significance" for the property that a word has when it means, and the word "signification" for that which is meant by it. To ask whether a certain notation has significance is to ask whether it means anything. To ask about a word's signification is to ask what is meant by it. A meaningless notation lacks all significance and has no signification. A word has both significance and signification. Its significance may be designative significance, signal significance, or operative significance (i.e., if the word happens to be a particle or linguistic operator instead of a name-word).

It would, therefore, appear to be the case that an ample enough vocabulary is available to avoid all the ambiguities which are latent in any discussion of the problem of meaning. This is not to say that in what follows I will always avoid using the word "meaning," always replacing it by some other word; but when I do use it, I can always make its meaning precise by accompanying its use with the parenthetical addition of one of these other words that is less ambiguous.

Before we leave this matter of substitutes for the word "meaning" in all of the various ways in which it can be used, one further point should be made; namely, that the various uses of a word are coextensive with its various meanings. Since a word is not a word unless it has meaning (significance), it cannot be used without being used to mean (signify) in one way or another; and in some cases, though not in all, it cannot be used without its use being determined by its meaning (its referent or sense). Hence, in my view, it is fatuous to think, as some appear to do, that the philosophical problem of meaning can be evaded by the empty recommendation "Don't look for the meaning; look for the use." To discover the ways in which a word is or can be used is to discover the ways in which it means or can mean (signifies), and the meanings that it has or can have (its senses or significations, and its significates or referents).

Question 6. Does the eulogistic use of the word "meaningful" and the dyslogistic use of the word "meaningless" raise a problem for the philosophy of language?

When, in the sphere of language, the words "meaningless" and "meaningful" are used descriptively, not normatively, they are used to draw a line of demarcation between (i) mere physical notations which have not yet become words because they lack meaning (nonsense syllables, such as "glub" and "smish," or "fronteraly" and "nagawappy") and (ii) notations that have become words in virtue of the meanings that they have acquired. Accordingly, no word can be meaningless, and no mere physical notation can be meaningful in any of the ways in which a word is meaningful.

Until the seventeenth century, the words "meaningless" and "meaningful," or substitutable words such as "insignificant" and "significant," were employed in the descriptive manner indicated above. Another use of "meaningless" and "meaningful" was introduced by an English philosopher at the beginning of modern times. That other use lapsed for the next two centuries, only to be reintroduced again in the twentieth century, with great vigor and insistence, by philosophers concerned with language. That new use of the two words is eulogistic and dyslogistic in the following manner: it identifies having meaning or being meaningful with having the value of truthfulness; and it identifies lacking meaning or being meaningless with falsity, or lacking the value of truthfulness.

One example, drawn from the seventeenth-century discussion of the point, should suffice to illustrate what is happening here. The philosopher who introduced this eulogistic and dyslogistic distinction, was, in his own view of reality, a full-fledged materialist in the tradition of the ancient atomists. In the view he espoused, nothing really exists except atoms and the void, or the composite bodies—the corporeal substances—that are made up of atoms and the void. He came to his consideration of language with this prior ontological commitment; and in consequence of it, he quite correctly observed that many words or phrases, both in ordinary speech and in philosophical discourse, do not signify or refer to bodies, either simple or composite. Since he believed that nothing but bodies really exist, such words or phrases signify or refer to nothing that exists in reality or can really exist. It was a simple but fallacious step on his part to conclude that such words or phrases (e.g., "angel" or "incorporeal substance") signify or refer to nothing; and so he called them "meaningless," "senseless," or "nonsensical speech."

It should be apparent at once that the word "angel" is not meaningless in the way that the nonsense syllable "glub" or "nagawappy" is. If it were, the question whether or not angels really exist could not even be raised, and the materialist could not conclude, on the basis of his premises, that it is impossible for angels to exist in reality. Neither he nor any else would ask whether or not glub really exists, or conclude that nagawappy cannot exist in reality. The reason for this difference is that "angel," unlike "glub" and "nagawappy," is not meaningless, senseless, or nonsensical speech.

It is, therefore, evident that the dyslogistic use of the word "meaningless" can be applied only to words that are "meaningful" in the descriptive sense of that adjective. Only words (i.e., only meaningful or significant notations, not meaningless ones such as nonsense syllables) can be either meaningless or meaningful in the additional dyslogistic or eulogistic sense which involves truth or falsity. To understand how truth or falsity can be involved, it is necessary to ask how these values can be attributed to words. The immediate and inescapable answer is that they cannot be attributed to words or even to phrases, but only to sentences which are capable of being logically construed as propositions that are precise enough to be judged either true or false.

What, then, is intended when it is said that the word "angel" is meaningless in the dyslogistic sense of that term, which involves falsity? The amplification required to make the intention clear requires the use of the word "angel" in a sentence which can be logically construed as an existential proposition in which the word "angel" is supposed to stand for the subject term; viz., "angels do not have wings." (An equivalent affirmative statement would be "angels are wingless.") To construe either sentence as an existential proposition involves its being interpreted as the conjunction of two assertions: (i) angels exist, and (ii) angels do not have wings. Since, according to the belief or ontological commitment of the materialist, the first of these two assertions is false, the conjunction is also false. Here, then, is the falsity that is attributed to the word "angel" when it is dyslogistically called meaningless.

Naming is not asserting. The word "angel" may not name anything that really exists, but it certainly does name something that men can talk about to one another and, in addition, can disagree about when they ask the question that certainly can be asked, "Do angels in fact really exist?" The use of the word "angel" as a name does not and cannot assert that angels really exist; if it did, we could not use the word, as we surely do, to ask whether or not angels really exist. There seems to be no way of escaping the conclusion that the dyslogistic use of the word "meaningless" is illegitimate or unjustifiable; worse it is thoroughly misleading, for it confuses meaningfulness with truth, and meaninglessness with falsity.

Whereas words are always meaningful or have significance

31

(otherwise, they would not be words in the lexicon of a language), phrases or sentences may be either significant or insignificant, according to the way in which words are put together in their construction. Even when they are significant, phrases, like words, are neither true nor false. Only significant sentences, and among significant sentences only those which can be construed as assertible propositions, are either true or false. Not all significant sentences are declarative in mood; questions, for example, and commands are neither true nor false. Not even all significant sentences which are declarative in mood and can be construed as assertible propositions are sentences which can be construed as existential affirmations or denials. Only such sentences and only those which are affirmative involve a word or phrase which, occupying the position of the subject term, must be construed as denoting something that really exists; if it cannot be so construed, the affirmative existential proposition is false.

The existential denotation of a name-word or designative phrase is something that is quite distinct from and additional to its referential significance. A word, such as "angel," can have referential significance without having existential denotation; otherwise we could not significantly ask whether angels do or do not really exist. If our view is that they do not, then the word lacks existential denotation (i.e., it denotes nothing that really exists); but in order for us to express that denial, we must be able to use the word "angel" significantly. We cannot do so unless it has a significate; and, since the word "angel" is a categorematic, not a syncategorematic, word, its significate must be a referent—something referred to, even though that something does not really exist. What that something is, and why it is not nothing even though it does not really exist, are questions that I cannot answer until Chapter IV, after I have presented, in Chapter III, a solution of the basic problem of meaning in the philosophy of language.

Here the only question to be answered is whether the eulogistic use of the word "meaningful" and the dyslogistic use of the word "meaningless' raise a problem for the philosophy of language. In the light of the foregoing analysis of the fallacy involved in employing "meaningful" and "meaningless" to connote truth and falsity, and of the confusion resulting from the failure to distinguish the designative or referential significance of name-words from their existential denotation, or lack of it, when they are construed as subject terms in affirmative existential propositions, I have no reluctance in saying that neither the dyslogistic use of the word "meaningless" nor the question about the existential denotation of words or phrases that function as the subject terms in affirmative existential propositions raise problems for the philosophy of language.

The confusion of existential denotation with referential significance in the case of categorematic words or name-words has led some contemporary philosophers to adopt positions that are certainly paradoxical if not plainly untenable. One is the position that only a word or phrase which is used in a sentence to express the subject term in a proposition construed from that sentence, has the referential or designative significance appropriate to a name; all the other categorematic words which are parts of the sentence refer to nothing; and if it is conceded that they have any meaning at all, which is not always acknowledged, the signification attributed to them is something like the mode of signification we have called "sense," the kind of meaning we have attributed to syncategorematic words or linguistic operators. An immediate consequence of this first position is the more extreme and even more questionable position held by some, that words or phrases in isolation have no meaning at all, and that only words or phrases used in sentences are meaningful.

One positive point, however, has emerged from the foregoing discussion. It consists in the distinction between referential meaning or significance and existential denotation. A name-word cannot function as a name without naming something. It must, therefore, have referential meaning or significance; but it need not have, in addition, the property of existential denotation; for what it refers to may be something that does not really exist.

It should also be pointed out that the existential denotation of a word is no part of its lexical meaning. It will not be included among all the meanings that are listed for it in a dictionary of the language. In this respect, existential denotation differs radically from the meanings of both categorematic and syncategorematic words, for all such meanings, and even in some cases the kind of meaning that we have called signal significance, are listed in the dictionary's report of a word's multiple significations. A given word may have both referential significance and syntactical significance (e.g., the word "is" used, on the one hand, as an existential predicate and, on the other, as an affirmative copula—a linguistic operator); and both of these significations will be found in the enumeration of that word's lexical meanings; but the dictionary does not and cannot tell us whether a given name-word denotes an entity that really exists. A biographical dictionary, the entries in which are proper names, may attempt to do that, but if and when it does, its statements involve existential assertions, either explicit or implied. An ordinary dictionary does not make such assertions. That is why existential denotations are not included among the meanings that it enumerates for the words it contains.

Question 7. Of the several modes of meaning (i.e., of signifying) that we have so far considered, and of the various uses of the word "meaning" that we have so far indicated, which concern the philosophy of language in dealing with its primary problem?

To answer this question, let me recapitulate the several modes of signifying and the various uses of the word "meaning."

I have distinguished three modes of signifying applicable to words: (1) the mode of signifying that is primary in the use of categorematic words or name-words; these always have designative or referential significance; (2) the mode of signifying that is secondary and only sometimes present in the use of such words; namely, their use as signals or as having signal significance; and (3) the mode of signifying that belongs to syncategorematic words or linguistic operators, through which they have sense without having referential significance. All three modes of meaning concern the philosophy of language in dealing with its primary problem. Of these three modes of signifying, only the first and third are peculiar to words (cf. Question 4, *supra*).

I have also distinguished between meaningless notations and meaningful words, and it is only this descriptive distinction between the meaningless and the meaningful which is relevant to the basic problem

34

of meaning in the philosophy of language. In addition, I have called attention to a threefold division that is relevant to the concerns of a philosophy of language in dealing with its basic problem: (1) some words have sense, but do not have either referential significance or existential denotation; (2) some words have referential significance, but do not have existential denotation; and (3) some words have both referential significance and existential denotation. In this attempt to account for the meaning of words in a way that enables us to see how they can be instruments of communication, it will be necessary to explain (i) how a word can have sense without having referential significance, (ii) how a word can have referential significance without having existential denotation, and (iii) how a word can have both referential significance and existential denotation.

Three.
The Solution
of the Primary Problem

Preamble

*T*he problem to be solved is how meaningless notations, such as physical marks or sounds, acquire meaning and thus become words in the dictionary of a language, words having one or more statable meanings, in almost every case more than one. To be satisfactory, the solution of this problem must account for the use of language as an instrument of communication, functioning in a way that enables human beings to converse or discourse with one another about matters or items that are common objects of reference.

I have noted that not all the words that have lexical meaning in the dictionary of a language are words that have referential significance; some, I have pointed out, have syntactical significance, functioning as linguistic operators rather than as name-words (see Chapter II, Questions 4 and 7). In proposing a solution to the problem with which we are here concerned, I will initially restrict our attention to the acquisition of referential significance by meaningless notations. I will then try to extend the proposed solution to the acquisition of syntactical significance by meaningless notations that become syncategorematic words, such as the particles of a language.

Although the solution, as will become clear, involves acts of the mind—acts of perception, memory, imagination, and thought, as well as acts of will—it does not attempt to explain how an individual human being learns a language, or how, in his individual case, this or that meaningless notation acquires the one or more meanings it may come to have for him. Although the solution attempts to account for the coming to be of meaningful words, it is genetic only in a philosophical, not a historical, manner; it will point out the factors that must be operative in every case in order for any meaningless notation to become a meaningful word, but it will not attempt to trace the actual steps by which any particular notation becomes a word.

To point out the factors that must be operative in order to account for the acquisition of meaning will inevitably raise further questions—questions about what is involved in the existence and operation of the factors mentioned. These further questions will lead us to consider the philosophical underpinnings of the solution here proposed. The consideration of them will be postponed until Chapter IV; and, until then, certain refinements in terminology cannot be achieved. In this chapter, I will present a bare and, in certain respects, rough statement of the solution that I regard as the only tenable and satisfactory solution of the problem. The reader is asked to table for the time being the further questions that arise in his mind as he examines the solution.

In this chapter, I will try to answer the following questions: 1. Can meaningless notations acquire referential significance without the intervention of mind? 2. Can meaningless notations acquire referential significance by being imposed on things? 3. Can meaningless notations acquire referential significance by being imposed on ideas? 4. Why is it that meaningless notations can acquire referential significance in no other way than by being imposed on the objects of perception, memory, imagination, and thought? 5. Do meaningful words ever function in the acquisition of referential significance by meaningless notations? 6. How do the meaningless notations that become syncategorematic words acquire their syntactical significance, and how does that mode of meaning differ from the referential significance of categorematic words or name-words?

Question 1. *Can meaningless notations acquire referential significance without the intervention of mind?*

It is necessary to explain the question before attempting to answer it. The word "mind" is here being used in the broadest possible sense to cover acts of perception, memory, imagination, and thought, and also to cover acts that are voluntary as contrasted with the involuntariness of purely reflex or automatic behavior. This use of the word "mind" does not commit us initially to any view of the relation of mind to brain as somehow distinct from one another. It does, however, preclude the complete reduction of mind to brain.

If (i) brain states or processes are regarded as being nothing but neurochemical conditions or events, and if (ii) they can be described in no other terms, and if (iii) it cannot be said that brain states or processes involve or give rise to acts of perception, memory, imagination, and thought (acts which are at least analytically distinct from brain states and processes described in neurochemical terms), then "mind" is just another word for "brain," and the use of it is misleading for it tends to suggest the addition of something somehow distinct.

If, however, mind is regarded as somehow distinct from brain, so that brain states or processes, in addition to being described in neurochemical terms, can be said to involve or give rise to acts of perception, memory, imagination, and thought, then mind can be appealed to as a factor in explaining the acquisition of referential significance by meaningless notations. This is the case whether brain states or processes are both the necessary and sufficient condition of acts of perception, memory, imagination, and thought, or only the necessary but not the sufficient condition of their occurrence.

To answer the question here being considered, we must, therefore, examine theories of human behavior in which mind is not in any way admitted as a factor distinct from brain, or, more generally, from the operation of the whole nervous system, peripheral as well as central.

All such theories, though they differ in particular respects, have enough in common to be collectively called "behavioristic." The question with which we are concerned thus becomes the question whether behavioristic theories can explain how meaningless notations become meaningful words by acquiring referential significance.

The answer to that question is negative, for a number of reasons. The first reason lies in the fact that behavioristic explanations are necessarily limited to accounting for the connections between physical stimuli, activating sense-organs, and muscular responses, activated by nervous impulses. Both the activation of sense-organs by physical stimuli and the activation of muscular responses by nervous impulses involve the action of the peripheral nervous system, though the sense-organs may not be on the surface of the body, receptive to stimulation from without, and though the muscular responses may not give rise to overt behavior by the organism, which is observable from without. The central nervous system (i.e., higher and lower brain centers and the spinal cord), according to behavioristic theory, comes into play as an elaborate connective mechanism, mediating between stimulus and response. If anything other than this connective function is attributed to the central nervous system, especially the higher brain centers, then the resultant theory ceases to be behavioristic in the radical sense of that term with which we began; this is certainly the case if the additional functions attributed to the brain involve acts of perception, memory, imagination, and thought as somehow distinct from neurochemical states or processes.

Limited to accounting for the connections between stimuli and responses, with the central nervous system functioning solely as a connective mechanism, behavioristic theory, in any of its forms, cannot explain how meaningless notations become meaningful words that have referential significance. The connections between stimuli and responses are either part of the innate endowment of the organism as its original, unconditioned reflexes, or they are learned connections, acquired through conditioning. Conditioned responses, according to behavioristic theory, involve the substitution of one stimulus for another, the substitute stimulus eliciting the response that was formerly elicited by the stimulus for which it is substituted. A meaningless notation might thus become the substitute stimulus eliciting a response that was formerly elicited by a nonverbal stimulus, as in the case of Pavlov's dog the sound of a bell became a substitute stimulus eliciting the salivary response formerly elicited by the sight cf food. The substitution is effected by the conjunction of the two stimuli and, through this, by the establishment of a connection between the substitute stimulus and the response which it acquires through this conditioning process.

What a theory of this sort may be able to explain is how a stimulus can function as a signal; for example, the sound of the bell signalling the imminence of food. The only evidence that the behaviorist can point to in support of this is the response which the organism makes to the substitute stimulus: because the dog salivates at the sound of the bell, that sound is regarded as a signal or cue that food is imminent, just as, by association or conditioning, the sound of the dinner-bell signals to human beings that dinner is ready; or just as smoke signals fire, or clouds signal rain. In all these cases, a nonverbal physical event, either man-made, as the ringing dinner-bell, or natural, as the clouds or smoke, becomes through association the signal of another physical event; and in all these cases, if we proceed in completely behavioristic terms, we can regard one physical event as the signal of another only if it elicits an observable response that is appropriate to the event being signalled.

What is to be explained, however, is referential significance, not signal significance, and the acquirement of such significance by physical notations that become name-words. The word "dinner" has referential significance whether the individual human being, upon hearing it, overtly or covertly behaves in one way or another: on hearing "dinner," he may remain immobile, move toward a dining room, or away from it. Similarly, women, seeing the word "Men" affixed to a door, usually respond in a manner quite opposite to the way in which men respond to the same visual stimulus. Yet the word "dinner" and the word "men" have, respectively, the same referential significance in all these cases of disparate behavior. Hence the range of responses, usually different and often opposed, that a word elicits or tends to elicit in human behavior, cannot be made the basis for explaining how the physical notation which became that word acquired its referential

41

significance. Furthermore, as we pointed out earlier, such words as "fire" or "dinner" function as signals that can be substituted for fire-bells or dinner-bells only in consequence of their having designative or referential significance as name-words. Since behavioristic theory cannot explain how, through the mechanism of substitute stimulus and conditioned response, a physical notation can acquire designative or referential significance, it cannot even explain how meaningful words can function as signals.

Take, for example, the nonsense syllable "glub"—a meaningless notation. Let it be an auditory stimulus associated with fire as a visual stimulus. Let the first conditioned response to fire be a withdrawing movement, resulting from the pain produced by coming too close to the heat. Suppose, further, that this conditioned response is now connected to the sound "glub" by its conjunction with the sight of fire. The organism reacts to glub by making an observable movement of withdrawal. Does this entitle us to say that "glub" has become the name of fire, designating or naming it when fire is not at the same time stimulating the individual's sense-organs? I think not. The reason is that a word possessing designative significance can be understood in exactly the same way by two men who, upon hearing it, react in opposite ways. A substitute stimulus, possessing only signal significance, cannot evoke opposite patterns of behavior in two organisms unless it has acquired that double significance through opposite processes of conditioning.

A second reason for dismissing behavioristic theory as incapable of solving the problem of how meaningless notations acquire referential significance lies in the fact that, even if it could explain the meaning of name-words that designate or refer to physical stimuli (which, as we have seen, it cannot do), it would find it impossible even to propose an explanation for the referential significance of words that name entities or items that do not and cannot function as physical stimuli activating sense-organs. A nonsense syllable, such as "glub," cannot become a stimulus that is substituted through conditioning for what is not a stimulus. Yet the dictionary of any language is full of words that refer to entities or items that cannot stimulate sense-organs; and these words were initially meaningless notations which have not only acquired referential significance, but also elicit a variety of observable responses and most frequently no observable response at all. How could these words have acquired their referential significance through the process of conditioning as formulated in behavioristic theory? In my judgment, there is no satisfactory answer to this question.

A third reason for dismissing behavioristic theory is that the meanings we find in the dictionary of a language are conventional. A large number of them, if not all, have resulted from voluntary decisions to use a physical notation in this way or that. Such voluntary decisions are sometimes made manifest by the declaration of a particular writer or speaker that he wishes to use a given notation in a certain, clearly specified way. He begs us to go along with him in employing the given notation with the designative or referential meaning that he wishes to assign to it. If behavioristic theory could account for the acquirement of meaning, either on the part of a totally meaningless notation or on the part of a word that already has certain meanings but not the one it is now about to acquire, it would nevertheless be baffled by voluntary decision as a factor in the acquirement of meaning. Though the unconditioned reflex may differ from the conditioned response as innate from learned behavior, the one does not differ from the other as involuntary from voluntary behavior. The conditioned response is just as involuntary as the unconditioned response.

For all these reasons, behavioristic theory fails to solve the problem that is the primary problem for a philosophy of language which aims to account for the communicative use of language. It fails because it omits mind as a factor, and especially the acts of perception, memory, imagination, and thought, and the making of voluntary decisions. However, it should be reiterated that if behavioristic theory regards the function of the brain as more than a connective mechanism between stimulus and response (that is, if it attributes to brain states or processes the aforementioned acts), then it also allows for the intervention of mind as a factor that can be appealed to in explaining how meaningless notations become meaningful words.

Such a modified and attenuated behaviorism might be able to explain how, through cumulative associative experience, a physical stimulus such as the natural phenomenon of smoke can become meaningful as a signal of fire; and, similarly, how a fire-bell can acquire the same signal significance for some individuals after others have adopted it as a signal by convention; but it would have to be modified still further, to a point where it would cease to be recognizable as behaviorism, in order for it to explain how the originally meaningless notation "fire" acquired its designative significance as a name-word; and, through that, became able, secondarily, to function as a signal.

Question 2. Can meaningless notations acquire referential significance by being imposed on things?

The theory that meaningless notations acquire referential significance by being imposed upon things as if they were labels is simplistic in the extreme. Yet, as compared with the behavioristic theory that I rejected in Question 1, it does make one advance toward a correct solution of the problem. It does acknowledge the activity of mind in at least one respect.

The various meanings that the dictionary of a language attaches to its words are all conventional. Anything that is conventional in human affairs is the product of voluntary institution by human beings: it could have been otherwise, had men willed it so. The theory with which we are here concerned recognizes this fact, as behaviorism does not, by introducing the notion of voluntary imposition as a factor in the acquirement of referential meaning by initially meaningless notations. To this extent at least, an activity of mind intervenes in the process by which meaningless notations become meaningful words. But this step forward does not go far enough, for the theory under consideration either omits or does not take sufficient account of the mind's activity in apprehending things—its acts of perception and thought.

As a result of this omission, the theory proceeds as if names could be imposed on things by a labelling process conducted blindly without regard to our perception or understanding of the things being labelled. Let us employ the phrase "thing-as-such" for a physical thing which exists independently of the human mind and is what it is regardless of whether or how it is apprehended by us. The theory under consideration would have us be able to give meaning to meaningless notations by affixing them as labels on things-as-such—this notation as the word which names this thing-as-such; that notation as the word which names that thing-as-such. To understand why this fails to solve the problem with which we are concerned, it is necessary to examine the difference between the thing-as-such and the thing-as-perceived, as well as the difference between the mere awareness of the sensible presence of the thing-as-such and the perception of that thing as an object.

Both of these differences are rooted in the difference between an individual and a particular. An individual is a unique one—that one and no other; but so long as it remains purely an individual, it is not one of a kind. In contrast, a particular, while also a unique one, is one of a kind, or one of this kind as well as one of that kind, for a particular may be one of many diverse kinds. It is only under extraordinary circumstances, or under controlled laboratory conditions, that we are ever aware of the sensible presence of an individual. In our normal experience, we are almost without exception aware of perceived particulars: not just this individual or that individual, but this particular man or that particular tree. When, in the sensible presence of this individual, we perceive it as a particular man, or in the sensible presence of that individual, we perceive it as a particular tree, our perception involves some understanding of the kind of thing that a man or a tree is; otherwise we could not perceive the individual as one of that kind. Our perception of individuals as particulars always involves acts of thought or understanding as well as the activation of the senses and also of the memory and the imagination.

With this clear, it should be readily apparent that the theory under consideration fails with respect to the referential significance of common names, such as "man" and "tree." The initially meaningless notation which became the word "man" could not have acquired its referential significance by being imposed on a thing-as-such—an individual pointed to or otherwise nonverbally indicated, of the sensible presence of which we are aware. That individual, when grouped with other individuals that are like it in certain respects, becomes a particular, one of a kind; and when grouped with still other individuals that are like it in certain other respects, it becomes still another particular, one of another kind. One and the same individual might thus be labelled a man, an animal, a biped, or a mammal, according to the respects in which it is grouped with other individuals and different particulars—one of this kind or one of that kind. Unless the individual ceases to be just an individual and becomes a particular, one of this kind or one of that kind, how can we affix to it the label "man," or the labels "animal," "biped," or "mammal"? Clearly, that is impossible to do. It follows, therefore, that meaningless notations cannot acquire their referential significance as common names by being imposed on things-as-such—on individuals rather than on perceived particulars.

While we are on this point, let us consider the meaning of such words as "this" and "that," and similar words such as "I" and "you." It would appear to be the case that, if such words are regarded as having referential meaning, they are indefinitely ambiguous; for "this" or "that" can refer to any individual which is being pointed to or otherwise indicated by bodily movement; and "I" and "you" can refer to any individual who is the person speaking or the person addressed. On the one hand, these words appear to have a definite meaning (e.g., the individual pointed to; the person speaking); on the other hand, each can be used to refer to an indefinite number of individuals. Hence it would appear to be the case that their definite meaning does not consist in what they designate or refer to.

The appearance is deceptive because of the failure to distinguish between referential meaning and existential denotation. Words like "this" and "that," "I" and "you," have one definite referential or designative meaning ("this" designates the individual being pointed to; "I" designates the person speaking); but they also involve an indefinite number of existential denotations when they are used by different individuals under different circumstances. They are systematically ambiguous with respect to their existential denotation, but quite unambiguous in their referential or designative significance.

It may, of course, still be asked what it is they mean, i.e., refer to or designate, if they do not refer to or designate any individual thing. The answer must wait until we come, in Question 4, to the solution of the problem of meaning, especially that part of the solution which concerns the character of that which is meant (the referent or significate) in the case of all words that have referential or designative significance.

Another question, and one that must be answered here, is whether we can ever impose a meaningless notation upon an individual—a thing-as-such—so that it acquires referential significance as the proper name of that one, unique individual, regarded just as an individual and not as a particular of any kind. The age-old and familiar ceremony of christening children would appear to be precisely such an act of labelling—of imposing a proper name on this one individual child, so that the initially meaningless notation thus imposed becomes a meaningful word having the referential significance of a proper, rather than a common, name. Again the appearance is deceptive, for we have failed to note that, in actual practise, we seldom if ever affix a proper name to an individual which we do not also denote by a definite description that particularizes it.

The individual that is given a proper name may be a human child or an animal adopted as a household pet. Let the proper name be "Toby." In the one case, the individual that "Toby" existentially denotes is also denoted by the definite description "the first son of Mr. and Mrs. Harold Jones, born December 8, 1972." In the other case, the individual that "Toby" existentially denotes is also denoted by the definite description "the Airedale puppy adopted by Mr. and Mrs. Harold Jones, on December 8, 1972, having the ancestry stated in the attached kennel record." (In each case, the definite description could be made more precise by the addition of details that perfectly identified the unique individual being existentially denoted.) When it is seen that the proper name "Toby" can be synonymous with two quite different definite descriptions (i.e., "Toby" has the same existential denotation that two different definite descriptions also have), it is clear that "Toby" is not a pure proper name—the name of a unique individual that is not a particular of any kind.

It is highly questionable whether, in actual usage, there are any pure proper names (or, as they are sometimes called, "logically" proper names), waiving the question whether it is possible to prove, in principle, that there cannot be a pure or logically proper name. If, then, in actual usage, a definite description can always be substituted for a proper name, proper names do not refer to individuals (things-as-such), but to particulars; and so the imposition of proper names always involves acts of the mind—acts of perception and understanding. Hence the theory that meaningless notations can acquire referential meaning by being imposed on things-as-such fails in the case of proper names as much as it fails in the case of common names, and for the same reason; namely, that, except for the volitional act of imposition, the theory omits acts of the mind—especially the acts of perception and thought.

Before we leave the matter of proper names, one other point should be made. A pure or logically proper name, if there ever were one, would be a proper name for which no definite description could be substituted in virtue of the fact that it had the same existential denotation as the proper name in question. In contrast, for proper names as actually used in everyday speech, one or more definite descriptions can always be substituted because they have the same existential denotation. This raises the question whether proper names and the definite descriptions which can be substituted for them are synonymous in their referential significance as well as in their existential denotation. The answer is that an ordinary proper name can be ambiguous in its referential significance, since a number of different definite descriptions can be substituted for it in virtue of their all having the same existential denotation as the proper name in question. Each of these different definite descriptions will have a different referential significance while having the same existential denotation; i.e., it will denote one and the same individual which is being referred to as a different particular in each instance—as being one of this kind or one of that kind.

The answer just given is closely related to the answer given earlier to the question about the meaning of "this" and "that," "I" and "you." In that case, we saw that each of the words under consideration had one and the same referential significance while being systematically ambiguous in its existential denotation. In this case, we see that a proper name and the various definite descriptions that can be substituted for it have one and the same existential denotation while differing in their referential significance. The further question concerning the character of the different referents, which differ not only from the individual thing that is being existentially denoted but also from each other, must be postponed until we come, in Question 4, to the solution of the problem of referential meaning.

There is an additional reason why the theory being considered fails to solve that problem. Even if it could account for the acquisition of referential meaning by meaningless notations in terms of their being imposed on things-as-such (individual existing things that are not perceived as particulars), the theory under examination cannot account for the acquisition of referential meaning by meaningless notations, when those notations become meaningful words that refer to items or entities that are *not* physical things which are sensibly present and capable of being pointed to or otherwise indicated. Either (i) such words as "justice" and "freedom," "infinity" and "asymptote," "mind" and "thought," and a vast host of similar words in the dictionary of a language, do not have referential meaning; or (ii) the referential meaning they do have cannot be explained by the theory under consideration.

On the first of these alternatives, such words would either have to be meaningless, in which case they would not be in a dictionary; or the meaning they do possess would have to be the kind of syntactical meaning that is possessed by such words as "the" and "a," "and," "or," "but," "is," "not," "of," "to," and "by." Clearly, that cannot be the case, for words like "justice" and "freedom," "infinity" and "asymptote," are not linguistic operators. They are as much name-words as "Toby," "man," and "tree." Hence the theory under consideration cannot account for the acquisition of referential meaning by meaningless notations that become name-words.

Question 3. Can meaningless notations acquire referential significance by being imposed on ideas?

The theory rejected in the answer to Question 2 made at least one advance toward the solution of the problem, by introducing voluntary imposition as a factor in the acquisition of referential significance. In this respect, it corrected one of the mistakes of behaviorism, which wrongly supposes that the acquisition of referential significance can be explained by conditioning rather than by voluntary imposition.

The theory to which we now turn would appear to go further toward the solution of the problem by introducing not only voluntary imposition as a factor in the acquisition of referential significance, but also cognitive acts of the mind, such as the acts of perception, memory, imagination, and thought. If the intervention of mind in the process whereby a meaningless notation becomes a meaningful name-word is required for a satisfactory solution of the problem, a theory that introduces the aforementioned cognitive acts as well as the volitional act of imposition would appear to provide the solution we are seeking.

That, however, is not the case. To explain the failure of a theory which makes ideas the referents or significates of name-words, and which, therefore, holds that meaningless notations become meaningful name-words by being imposed on ideas, it is necessary to be clear about how the word "idea" is used in such a theory. An act of the mind, such as perceiving or perception, results in a product—a percept. Similarly, an act of thought, conceiving, or understanding, results in a concept; and the same can be said for the acts of memory or remembering and the acts of imagination or imagining: they produce memories and images.

I have not mentioned sensing and sensations, for two reasons. (i) Sensing is a passive reception by the mind rather than an action on its part; consequently, sensations are received impressions, not products of the mind's activity. (ii) Sensations, as received impressions, forming the sensory core or sensory input of our sense-perceptions, cannot be isolated as identifiable elements of experience, except perhaps under the most rigorously controlled laboratory conditions.

Sense-perception does not occur without sense-impressions or sensory input, but neither does it consist exclusively in the having of sensations. It involves a constructive act of the mind, the product of which is a percept. Perception is no less a constructive act of the mind than memory, imagination, and conception or thought. The products of these several acts—percepts, memories, images, and concepts—can all be grouped together under the term "idea," just as all the acts by which they are produced can be grouped together under the term "acts of the mind." (In the theory under consideration, sensations are also called ideas, even though they are clearly not products of the mind's activity.)

The acts of the mind so far mentioned can all be grouped together under the generic term *apprehension*, just as the diverse products of these different acts can all be grouped together under the generic term *idea*. Employing the words "apprehension" and "apprehending" in this generic sense, we can say that the acts of perceiving, remembering, imagining, and conceiving, are all acts of apprehending or acts of apprehension. As these different acts of apprehension differ, so do the ideas which are their products.

Acts of apprehension are not the only cognitive acts of the mind. There are, in addition, acts of judging and of reasoning. It is important at this point to note one extremely important difference between apprehending and judging, or between their respective products—ideas and judgments. Ideas as such are neither true nor false. Only judgments—affirmations or denials—are either true or false. Hence to call both apprehending and judging cognitive acts or acts of knowledge is to use the words "cognitive" and "knowledge" ambiguously. The latent equivocation can be avoided only by carefully noting that the meaning of the word "knowledge" is not the same when it is said of an apprehension and when it is said of a judgment. Those who identify expressions of knowledge with statements which are true, and expressions of error with statements which are false, may have a certain understandable reluctance about calling an act of apprehension knowledge; but since it is difficult if not impossible to thus restrict the use of the word "knowledge," it is all the more necessary to avoid using the word equivocally by always explicitly noting the shift in its meaning when it is applied to apprehensions, on the one hand, and to judgments, on the other.

With these matters clarified, we can now call attention to the two major defects of the theory which maintains that meaningless notations acquire the referential significance of name-words by being voluntarily imposed on ideas—defects which prevent it from providing a satisfactory solution of the problem.

The first defect lies in the fact that, according to the theory under consideration, each individual has his own ideas. The ideas in the mind of one individual are numerically and existentially distinct from the ideas in the mind of another. If a given individual ceased to exist, his ideas would cease to exist with him, for their existence is subjective in the sense that it is totally dependent on his existence as the subject who has them. Precisely because ideas are subjective in the sense indicated, making them the objects that are signified or referred to by the words which have been imposed on them as their names prevents language from being used as an instrument of communication. It can be so used, as we have repeatedly observed, only if its words refer to items or entities that are public rather than private—referents that are common to two or more persons engaged in conversation or discourse. Since ideas are subjective items or entities, they cannot be common referents, for they are private rather than public. Hence, although the theory under consideration may succeed in explaining how meaningless notations acquire referential significance by being imposed by an individual on his own ideas, and so become words that name, signify, or refer to those ideas, it is unsatisfactory because it necessarily fails to do what is required of a satisfactory solution of the problem; namely, to explain the acquisition of meaning in a way that also accounts for the use of language as an instrument of communication.

It must be acknowledged at once that the theory being criticized recognizes the fact that language is used as an instrument of communication. It must, further, be acknowledged that the theory being criticized recognizes the difficulty arising from that fact, in view of its own admission that the ideas in a given individual's mind, to which his name-words refer, are subjective. Finally, it must be acknowledged that the theory being criticized tries to overcome this difficulty by suggesting that the subjective ideas in one individual's mind are sufficiently like the subjective ideas in another individual's mind, so that communication between them can occur even though the words they use refer to or signify objects that are not identical and, therefore, not common objects of reference for both of them. This cannot be dismissed as having no merit whatsoever, but it leaves the acknowledged fact of communicative discourse as something of a mystery that is not fully explained.

III. *Solution of the Primary Problem*

The second defect of the theory under consideration lies in the fact that, according to it, ideas and nothing but ideas are the objects of our apprehension as well as the objects referred to or signified by our name-words. Since name-words can refer to or signify only that which we apprehend, and since ideas are solely that which we apprehend, name-words can only refer to or signify ideas. Nevertheless, the theory being criticized acknowledges that men discourse or converse about the real things that comprise the world in which they live, not just their own subjective ideas. Men assert that one thing or kind of thing really exists, and that another does not. Men ask whether a certain thing or kind of thing exists. How can they possibly do this if the name-words they use refer to or signify nothing but their own ideas?

Once again it must be noted that the theory being criticized confesses that this fact raises a difficulty for it, which it tries to overcome by suggesting that just as an individual's name-words signify the ideas in his own mind on which he has imposed them, so those subjective ideas in turn signify or refer to the things—the real existences—which have somehow been the cause of his having those ideas in the first place. This suggestion, like the previous one made to overcome the earlier embarrassment, fails, and fails even more obviously.

In the first place, it leaves unexplained how an idea, which is the significate or referent of the name-word that is imposed on it, can at the same time function as a signifier that designates or refers to things that are not objects of apprehension. In the second place, human discourse frequently involves questions about the real existence or nonexistence of certain entities, as well as assertions that certain entities do not exist. Such questions and assertions cannot be explained even if our subjective ideas did somehow refer to or signify things that really exist; for the entities being referred to in such questions or assertions are clearly not our own ideas nor are they always really existing things. In the third place, even if the suggestion under consideration could explain how our name-words signified both ideas as their immediate objects of reference and also things as their mediated objects of reference (mediated by the functioning of ideas as referential signs), it could not explain how certain name-words have existential denotation as well as referential significance while other name-words have referential significance without existential denotation. It is prevented from solving these aspects of the problem by its resolute commitment to the proposition that ideas, and only ideas, are the objects which we apprehend when we perform any of the acts that have been called acts of apprehending, as contradistinguished from acts of judgment or reasoning; i.e., acts of perceiving, remembering, imagining, and understanding or conceiving.

That proposition is the crucial and fatal error in the theory which attempts to explain the acquisition of referential meaning in terms of an individual's voluntary imposition of meaningless notations upon his own ideas as the objects to which they refer. The error is corrected when we commit ourselves to exactly the opposite proposition; namely, that an individual's own subjective ideas are never the objects which he apprehends. They are never, and cannot be, the objects he apprehends when he perceives, remembers, imagines, or thinks. If this is so, an individual's own subjective ideas cannot be the objects to which his name-words refer, for he cannot refer to that which he cannot apprehend. Consequently, meaningless notations cannot become meaningful name-words by being imposed on subjective ideas.

Since they cannot be either things-as-such or subjective ideas, what, then, are the objects of reference which our name-words signify or designate, and upon which meaningless notations must be voluntarily imposed in order for them to become meaningful words that have referential significance? The answer sought for is the answer to Question 4, which follows.

Question 4. Why is it that meaningless notations can acquire referential significance in no other way than by being imposed on the objects of perception, memory, imagination, and thought?

We have seen that the acquisition of meaning cannot be explained in a way that accounts for the communicative use of language either in terms of the voluntary imposition of notations upon individual things-as-such or upon subjective ideas—the ideas that each individual has in his own mind. Since the meanings that meaningless notations acquire to become the words of a language are conventionally instituted, we have also seen that an explanation of the acquisition of meaning must involve voluntary imposition. If not upon individual things-as-such and not upon subjective ideas, then voluntary imposition on what?

The answer involves acts of the mind, such as perception, memory, imagination, and thought, as well as their products, i.e., ideas; but it is by imposition on the objects which we apprehend by means of those ideas, not by imposition on the ideas themselves, that meaningless notations acquire their referential significance. Here, in germ, is the solution of the problem with which we are concerned. To claim that it is the only solution, that there is no other way of explaining how meaningless notations acquire referential meaning, is to assert, *first*, that no fourth alternative is available (i.e., that things-as-such, subjective ideas, and the objects of those ideas exhaust the entities that might be signified or referred to by words); and *second*, that the third alone of these alternatives affords an explanation of referential meaning that not only accounts for the use of language as an instrument of communication, but also avoids the embarrassments encountered by solutions which appeal to either one of the other two alternatives.

This is not to say that the theory to be presented is without certain difficulties. No theory is. But, as we have seen, the theories advanced in the answers to Questions 2 and 3 do not succeed in overcoming the difficulties which they engender. It remains to be seen whether the present theory can succeed where the others have failed. Finding out whether or not it can must be postponed until Chapter V. Here I shall confine myself to explicating the theory which has so far been only barely indicated.

The basic proposition upon which the theory rests is that ideas (percepts, memories, images, and concepts) are that by which we apprehend whatever we apprehend, and never the objects of our apprehension—that which we apprehend. Stated another way, the proposition is that the subjective ideas in an individual's mind are always and solely the means whereby he apprehends something other than his own ideas, and never something that he is able to apprehend or be aware of in any manner or degree. He cannot experience his own ideas; they are totally uninspectable by him; he has no awareness of them. This does not preclude his knowing, by inference from effects to their causes, that subjective ideas really exist. We have inferential knowledge of many things of which we have no direct experience.

The individual experiences perceived objects, but never the percepts whereby he perceives them; remembered objects, but never the memories by which he remembers them; imagined or imaginary objects, but never the images by which he imagines them; and objects of conceptual thought, but never the concepts by which he thinks or conceives them.

The objects that the individual experiences through the acts of his mind and by means of the ideas that such acts produce may or may not exist in reality or have instantiation in reality. For example, the objects that we remember may once have really existed but no longer exist; the objects that we imagine may have had no real existence in the past, may not really exist at present, and may never come to have such existence; and the objects of thought may be such that we raise questions about their actual existence or their instantiation in reality, or about the possibility of their having such existence or instantiation. Even in the case of perception, we may, under unusual circumstances, confuse imaginary and perceived objects. For example, the object of an hallucination may be regarded as an object being perceived when, in fact, it is not.

Whether or not the objects we apprehend by means of our ideas really exist or have instantiation in reality does not affect the role that the objects of our apprehension play in conferring referential significance upon words; i.e., as the referents to which they refer, the significates which they designate or name. Naming, as we have pointed out, is not asserting. For a word to name one or another object that we apprehend does not by itself assert or deny the real existence of the object apprehended or its instantiation in reality.

The distinction we made earlier between apprehending and judging (together with their products, ideas and judgments) is paralleled by the grammatical distinction between names (or descriptive phrases) and sentences, and by the logical distinction between terms and propositions. Assertions (affirmations or denials) are verbally expressed in declarative sentences; such sentences can be logically construed as affirmative or negative propositions; and when we assert a proposition, we do so by an act of the mind that is an act of judgment, not of apprehension. When we simply name something, we are not asserting anything; we are not judging, and since we are not judging, questions of truth and falsity do not arise. Only propositions, expressed in sentences, are either true or false, not terms, expressed in words or phrases.

An object named is not an object asserted to exist; on the contrary, it is, in principle, always an object the real existence of which is to be questioned. Though that question is, in principle, always applicable, it is not always applied in fact, especially not to the objects of perception (see Chapter V, Question 2). When it is applied, however, the answer always takes the form of an existential proposition or assertion, expressed verbally in a declarative sentence, never in a name-word or a descriptive phrase by itself. What is thus expressed verbally in a declarative sentence, and has the logical form of an assertible proposition, expresses a judgment of the mind which is an act of knowledge, or an act which claims to be knowledge, because it claims to be true, though, of course, it may in fact be false.

To hold a view contrary to the one that has just been expounded would be tantamount to saying that we cannot remember, imagine, or think of (i.e., conceive) objects that do not really exist or that do not have instantiation in reality, which is plainly contrary to common experience. It is equally at odds with common experience to assert or imply that we cannot name or refer to, either by single words or by descriptive phrases, whatever objects we are able to remember, imagine, or conceive, whether or not they really exist or have instantiation in reality. We can avoid such absurdities only by holding fast to the view that we can name or designate (by single words or descriptive phrases) whatever objects we are able to apprehend by means of our ideas; and this is inseparable from the view that we can never apprehend our own ideas, since they are not the objects which we apprehend but only the instruments or means by which we apprehend objects. These two theses, taken together, lie at the heart of the theory that meaningless notations acquire the referential or designative significance by which they become name-words by being voluntarily imposed on the objects we are able to apprehend by means of our percepts, memories, images, and concepts.

If the objects of our ideas were as subjective as those ideas themselves, the theory that we are proposing would fail for exactly the same reason that the theory fails which maintains that the name-words an individual uses signify his own ideas and nothing but his own ideas, exclusively private or locked within the confines of his own experience. If that were so, communication would be impossible. The individual could not use language to convey his ideas to anyone else; nor could two individuals converse with one another about entities or items to which they are both able to refer.

Hence it follows that, whatever mode of being we assign to the objects which we apprehend by means of our ideas, it cannot be the kind of subjective existence that belongs to the ideas which are the products of our mind's activity. Nor can it be the mode of being which we speak of as existence in reality, for that which really exists is that which exists whether or not it is in any way apprehended or known by us. Real existence is totally independent of the acts of the human mind; as, at the opposite extreme, the kind of subjective existence that belongs to ideas is totally dependent on the acts of individual minds, the ideas that each individual has, existing in his individual mind and only there.

In between these two extremes of real existence and subjective existence, of existence totally independent of the acts of the human mind and existence totally dependent on the acts of an individual mind, what middle ground is there? The answer which, though stated here, cannot be fully explicated until later (see Chapter IV, Question 3), employs an analytical term that has a certain currency in modern philosophical thought; namely, *intersubjectivity*. To say that the objects we apprehend and name are intersubjective is to say that they are one and the same objects for two or more individuals, even though each individual apprehends them by means of his own subjective ideas, products of the acts of his own individual mind.

Two individuals can perceive the same object even though they do not and cannot have one identical percept; they can remember the same object, even though they do not have one identical memory. They can imagine one and the same object, even if the subjective image in the mind of one and the subjective image in the mind of the other are two existentially and numerically distinct images, each existing in one individual's mind and only there. So, too, they can conceive or think of one and the same object, even though the concepts which have subjective existence in the minds of each individual are existentially and numerically distinct.

If this were not so, two individuals could not talk to one another about one and the same perceived, remembered, or imagined object, or about one and the same object of thought. Their being able to converse or discourse about common or public objects—the fact which was our point of departure (see Chapter I, Question 1)—depends upon their being able to use words or descriptive phrases to name, refer to, or designate common or public objects of discourse. If the objects to which our name-words or descriptive phrases refer were subjective rather than intersubjective in the sense indicated, this would be impossible.

It is one thing to assert that something is the case, and another to explain how it can be the case. All I have done so far is to assert that two individuals can apprehend one and the same public object even though the two ideas by which they apprehend it are existentially distinct, each an idea private to the individual in whose mind it occurs. How this can be so is an extremely difficult problem which I think I can solve—or at least indicate the direction in which the solution lies.

The solution will be offered in the answer to Question 1 of Chapter V, after I have examined and defended in Chapter IV the several presuppositions of the theory being expounded. Here suffice it to say that the germ of the solution lies in this: while a particular idea in the mind of one individual and a particular idea in the mind of another are, as existentially distinct, always two in number, they *can* be one in intention; that is, they can intend one and the same object, and make it present to the minds of two individuals. It is precisely such intentionality which is to be explained in order to solve the difficult problem of how two individuals can have one and the same object before their minds as an object of reference, capable of being named and talked about by both of them, even though each individual has his own idea of it, and his own idea is the means by which he apprehends the object to which his speech refers.

Before I leave this point, it may be useful to add that objectivity and intersubjectivity are identical. Nothing should be called an object or regarded as having objectivity which is not capable of being an object common to two or more individuals. There are no private objects, only public ones. To speak of the ideas that each individual has privately in his own mind as the objects that he apprehends is a contradiction in terms, since ideas are subjective rather than intersubjective. It is also a contradiction in terms to speak of the thing-as-such (the thing as it exists unapprehended) as an object. It may have a certain public character in that two individuals may lift or carry the same really existing thing, and do so without any prior awareness of it; but the public character of a thing-as-such does not include its being public as an object of reference or discourse.

Tabling for the present the presuppositions underlying the theory here proposed, as well as the difficulties to which they give rise, let us turn our attention to the way in which the theory solves the problem of how meaningless notations acquire referential significance and so become meaningful name-words.

To say that subjective ideas are nothing but the means or instruments by which the mind apprehends objects is to say that the sole function of an idea is to present to the mind the object that the idea is a means of apprehending. That is precisely the function of any sign or signifier, whether it be a signal or a designator—to make present to the mind something other than itself. When clouds signal rain, or smoke signals fire, that is precisely what they do in virtue of their functioning as signs. So, too, that is precisely what the meaningful words "rain" or "fire" do when they function as signs, designating, not signalling, that to which they refer. They make present to the mind that which is named or referred to, just as clouds and smoke make present to the mind the rain and fire that they respectively signal.

There is one critical difference, however, between (i) the clouds which signal rain, (ii) the word "rain" which names or designates the phenomenon referred to, and (iii) the percept, memory, or concept of rain which presents rain to the mind as an object apprehended by an act of perception, memory, or thought.

(i) The cloud that signals rain, like the rain it signals, is a physical phenomenon, a natural event. It is what it is whether or not it signals rain; signalling rain is adventitious to its nature. Signalling rain is a meaning that is conferred on clouds only in human experience and only as a result of the cumulative observation of the conjunction or sequence of clouds and rain.

(ii) The initially meaningless notation which comes to be the word that names or designates rain, is, like the cloud, a physical phenomenon—a sound or a mark; but, unlike the cloud, it is a man-made, not a natural event. Nevertheless, it is what it is as a visible mark or an audible sound whether or not it ever becomes a word or ever becomes the name of rain. Designating or referring to rain is as adventitious to its physical existence as signalling rain is adventitious to the nature of clouds. Designating rain is a meaning that is conferred on that visible mark or audible sound only as a result of human intervention. Not only is the initially meaningless notation a man-made mark or sound; the meaning that it comes to have as a name-word is also conventional. That same mark or sound could have carried a different meaning; conversely, that meaning (i.e., reference to the phenomenon of rain) could have been carried by a different mark or sound, as is the case in fact in different languages.

(iii) The idea (whether it is a percept, memory, image, or concept) which presents rain to the mind as an object apprehended is a natural occurrence, like clouds and fire, not a man-made entity, like the visible mark or audible sound that men devise to function as a notation capable of becoming a word. Acts of perceiving, remembering, imagining, and conceiving may be psychological, not physical, phenomena, but in any case they are natural phenomena: they involve the activation of powers inherent in the nature of a sentient and intelligent organism. Not only are these acts natural phenomena, whether psychological or physical (i.e., acts of the brain), but their products are also natural phenomena. Ideas are not man-made works of art, nor are they instituted by human convention.

What is even more important is that the meaning of ideas is *not* adventitious to their nature, as the meaning of the clouds that signal rain or the meaning of the word "rain" that designates it is something extrinsically added to these entities. The meaning of the idea of rain (whether it is a percept, memory, image, or concept) is wholly intrinsic to it. When we say that the meaning of the idea of rain is wholly intrinsic to it, we are saying that the idea is nothing but that meaning. To be an idea is to mean or signify the object which that idea presents to the mind. To say that an idea is that by which we apprehend an object or that an object is that which is apprehended by an idea is tantamount to saying that an idea is related to its object as a sign is to its significate; to which we must add that the critical difference between an idea as a sign and all other signs, whether they are signals or designators, lies in the fact that ideas have no being or nature except to function as signs. Each idea is nothing but the meaning by which it signifies or presents an object other than itself to the mind.

Earlier (in Chapter II, Question 2), I briefly adverted to the distinction between natural and acquired meaning—the difference between being a meaning and having a meaning. Ideas are the only entities in the whole world which *are* meanings, i.e., they are signifiers and nothing but signifiers. Everything else that signifies in any way only *has* meaning, which it must acquire. That which *has* a meaning which it acquires can change in meaning, lose meaning, or gain it. But that which means by its very nature cannot change, lose, or gain the meaning it *is*.

To be a meaning or to mean by nature, rather than adventitiously, involves a natural relationship of signifying between that which means and that which is meant. Clouds have a natural relationship to rain, and fire to smoke, but that is a relation of cause to effect, not a relation of signifier to significate. Only ideas stand in a natural relation to their objects, as signifiers to significates. That is why each idea is a meaning and its object is also a meaning, the idea a meaning in the sense of that which means (a signifier) and its object a meaning in the sense of that which is meant (a significate).

We should never speak of the meaning *of* an idea, or *of* its object, as we speak of the meaning *of* clouds or the meaning *of* the word "rain"; for in the case of ideas and their objects, and only in that case, meaning is not something possessed, acquired, or subject to change as it is in the case of natural phenomena like clouds or smoke, and as it is also in the case of man-made words like "rain" and "fire." To be stringently precise, one should speak of the meaning (signifying) that *is* an idea, or the meaning (significate) that *is* its object. The fact that clouds and smoke are natural phenomena does not make them natural signifiers, nor does it make rain and fire natural significates. Only the idea of clouds or smoke is a natural signifier; only the object of that idea is a natural significate.

Let us suppose for the moment that the natural world did not contain ideas among its constituents. In that case, there would be nothing that naturally means and nothing that is naturally meant. Any entity that means would have to acquire whatever meaning it has, because that meaning would be adventitious to its nature as a physical phenomenon, whether it is a natural event such as clouds or rain or a man-made entity such as a visible mark or audible sound devised to become a word. Furthermore, any entity which is initially meaningless and which adventitiously comes to have meaning would have to acquire whatever meaning it comes to have from some other entity which already has some meaning. Meaning cannot be acquired from that which is itself meaningless, i.e., one meaningless notation cannot acquire meaning by standing in some relationship to another meaningless notation. However, a meaningless notation can acquire meaning by being put into relationship with words that already have meaning; but, as I have already pointed out, all the words in a dictionary, each of which was initially a meaningless notation, could not have acquired their meanings that way, for the words in a dictionary form a closed circle with no beginning or end (see Chapter II, Question 1).

For the meaningless to acquire meaning from the meaningful where the meaning of the latter is itself always an acquired meaning involves an endless regress or a vicious circle. If everything that had to acquire meaning in order to become meaningful had to acquire its meaning from something else of the same sort, which in turn had to acquire its meaning from something else which possessed meaning only adventitiously, and so on, the endless regression thus set up, or the vicious circle, would render the acquisition of meaning inexplicable and impossible. Hence, unless there are in the world some entities that naturally mean and some that are naturally meant, no other entities could ever acquire the adventitious meanings that they come to have. Ideas, as natural signifiers, and their objects, as natural significates, supply precisely what is needed to solve the problem of how meaning is acquired by initially meaningless man-made notations, how it is acquired by natural phenomena such as clouds and smoke, or how it is acquired by man-made signals such as dinner-bells and fire-bells.

The solution of the problem is not the same for the acquisition of referential or designative significance by meaningless notations that become name-words and for the acquisition of signal significance (i) by such natural phenomenal as clouds and smoke, (ii) by such man-made devices as dinner-bells and fire-bells, or even (iii) by such meaningful name-words as "dinner" and "fire." In the first of the three foregoing cases, the adventitious meaning derives directly from an experienced sequence or conjunction of the entities that come to be related as a signal to the signalled; it only indirectly depends upon the ideas that we have of these entities, presenting them as objects of apprehension. In the other two cases, the signal significance of the fire-bell or the word "fire" is established by convention.

In sharp contrast, the acquisition of referential or designative significance by meaningless notations that become name-words depends directly and wholly upon the ideas that we have and the objects that they present. It is through their being associated with ideas (as natural signifiers) that the meaningless notations become conventional signifiers, and it is through their being imposed upon the objects of our ideas (as natural significates) that the meaningless notations become name-words which have those objects as their acquired and conventional significates or referents.

A number of minor points should be noted before I complete a statement of the solution to the problem that concerns us. One is that the initially meaningless notation which is imposed on an object apprehended can be affixed to it as its name or designator only insofar as that physical notation is itself an object apprehended. A visible mark or an audible sound can exist as a physical phenomenon and yet be unapprehended. Only when it is an apprehended object can it be imposed on another apprehended object which becomes its significate or referent and which gives to it its acquired meaning as a name-word.

A second point to be noted is that, since the subjective idea by which an object is apprehended is itself intrinsically and totally inapprehensible by the individual in whose mind it occurs and functions, a meaningless notation, even one that is itself apprehended as an object, cannot acquire its role as a signifier by being directly associated with the idea that functions naturally as a signifier. It is impossible for us to establish a direct association between two entities, one of which is an apprehended object (i.e., a seen mark or a heard sound) and the other of which cannot be apprehended at all (i.e., an idea).

With these points made, I can now summarize the solution in the following two statements. (i) A meaningless notation acquires its adventitious referential significance by being voluntarily imposed on an apprehended object as its name or designator. (ii) Through the repeated use of this name-word to refer to the object of an idea, it becomes indirectly associated with the idea which is the natural signifier of that object.

The initially meaningless notation can acquire meaning only by being imposed *directly* on an object that is actually being apprehended—an object that is present to the mind of the individual making the imposition. However, once it has acquired referential significance in this fashion and comes to possess it habitually by repetition, the resultant meaningful word, by evoking the idea (the natural signifier) with which it has been *indirectly* associated by repeated use as the name for the object of that idea, is able to make the object signified by that idea present to the mind of anyone who apprehends that word as having the particular meaning it thus acquired. The referential significance of words that were initially meaningless notations could not have been acquired without direct imposition upon the objects that are the natural significates of ideas; but, once acquired, the use of the word exercises that acquired meaning by evoking the idea, the natural signifier, with which it has become indirectly associated. Were this not the case, words having referential significance could not be used to bring before the mind of speaker or hearer the objects to which they adventitiously refer and which the ideas of those objects naturally signify.

Question 5. Do meaningful words ever function in the acquisition of referential significance by meaningless notations?

Two distinctions are involved in the answer to this question. The first is a distinction between (i) ideas which we have prior to and without the mediation of words, and (ii) ideas which arise in the mind as a result of the mind's understanding of meaningful words and, through that, the apprehension of the objects which they signify. The second distinction is one that has a certain currency in contemporary thought. It is the distinction between (i) knowledge by acquaintance and (ii) knowledge by description.

Unfortunately, most of the writers who have employed this second distinction have been careless in their use of the word "knowledge," which does not have the same meaning when applied to apprehension, on the one hand, and to judgment, on the other (see Question 3, supra). Upon examination of their writings, it appears that they are concerned with the apprehension of objects, not with judgments about reality—judgments about what is or is not the case. Properly stated, the point of this second distinction lies in the difference between those objects which we apprehend without the mediation of meaningful words and those which we apprehend through the mediation of meaningful words. Objects of the first sort, we can call "objects of acquaintance"; those of the second sort, we can call "objects of description," since they are apprehended as a result of the verbal description that is given of them.

The two distinctions are plainly parallel and related. On the one hand, objects of acquaintance are the objects of ideas which we have prior to and without the mediation of words. On the other hand, objects of description are the objects of ideas which arise in the mind as a result of its understanding of meaningful words. I can now answer the question with which we are here concerned by saying that whereas some meaningless notations must acquire referential significance by being imposed upon objects of acquaintance, it is not necessary for all meaningless notations to acquire their referential significance in that way. Some may acquire it by being imposed on objects of description; but here it must be added that all cannot acquire it in that way.

The reason for this has already been made clear; namely, that unless some meaningless notations acquire their referential significance by association, direct or indirect, with natural signifiers and natural significates, we are involved in an endless regress or vicious circle that makes the acquisition of meaning inexplicable and impossible (see Question 4, supra). However, given some meaningful words, it is possible for those words to be used descriptively in a way that permits a meaningless notation to acquire meaning by being imposed on the object that the meaningful words describe, that object having been presented to the mind by an idea that has been formed at the instigation of a verbal description.

Since the object that is named by a word which has acquired its meaning without the mediation of other words is an object of acquaintance, we shall speak of the designation of such objects as "naming by acquaintance." In contradistinction, when objects are named by words which have acquired their meaning only through the descriptive use of other words, we shall speak of the designation of such objects as "naming by description."

I can now restate the answer to the present question in the following manner. It is seldom if ever the case that all the meaningful words which an individual is able to use are words that have become meaningful for him through naming by acquaintance. To this it must be added that it is never the case that all the meaningful words which an individual is able to use are words that have become meaningful to him through naming by description; for in that case he would ultimately run out of the meaningful words he needs for descriptive purposes. What has just been said about naming by description in relation to naming by acquaintance repeats what is usually said about the relation of knowledge by acquaintance to knowledge by description; namely, that some knowledge by acquaintance is indispensable to there being any knowledge by description. The reverse is not true: we can have knowledge by acquaintance without having any knowledge by description.

It may be helpful to illustrate the analytical points that have just been made. We have all used words to describe an object of perception to another person who is not in the sensible presence of the thing that has become an object of perception for us. What is an object of acquaintance for us is an object of description for him—an object he is able to imagine as a result of the verbal description we have given him. Now let us suppose that our friend has never had direct acquaintance with that particular object before, and that his vocabulary does not include a name for it. Having described it to him, we then tell him the name we use to designate it. What would have been a meaningless notation before he heard our description of the object can now become a meaningful word for him, for he can impose it on the object described and use it as the name for that object.

The familiar ritual of social introductions provides an example of naming by acquaintance, in which a previously meaningless notation becomes a meaningful proper name. I meet a stranger at a party who, until I am introduced to him, is an unnamed object of acquaintance. Someone says "This is John Doe, the author of the novel that is over there on the table." This introduction permits me to impose "John Doe" on an object with which I was acquainted before I heard him named, and this enables me henceforth to use "John Doe" as a proper name for the individual whose hand I am now shaking.

Contrast that with an example of naming by description under the following circumstances. I listen to a conversation in which I hear mentioned what I can recognize to be a proper name even though I have no acquaintance with the individual being named. He has never entered my experience as an object of acquaintance. I gather from the context that the person being named is no longer alive and, in addition, that he was a person of some eminence when he lived. Uninformed about him by others at the time of the conversation, I subsequently go to a biographical dictionary and look up the proper name, and read a verbal description of the individual named. This verbal description enables me to imagine an object I have never perceived. My imagination having been instigated by the verbal description which I read in a dictionary of biography, I am now able to impose what was previously a meaningless notation on an object of description and use it as a proper name. Since the referential significance which that meaningless notation has thus acquired was mediated by a verbal description, what we have here is a case of naming by description.

Similar examples can be given in the case of common names, such as "man" or "tree," "justice" or "meson." Human beings are objects of acquaintance; they are objects of acquaintance through acts of perception, memory, and understanding or conception, whereby we apprehend individual human beings as particulars of a certain kind. When a child learns how to use the common name "man" as the designator of any and every perceived instance of that kind, or learns how to use it to refer to the kind itself even when no instance of the kind is being perceived, he usually does so by hearing the word "man" imposed on objects with which he is directly acquainted, and usually, though not always, without the mediation of verbal descriptions.

Verbal description may have to be introduced if the child makes the mistake of using the word "man" to name something that is not a human being. Meaningful words will then be used to define the kind or delimit the class so that the child will not henceforth misapply the word to instances that do not belong to it. Man, as a conceptual object or object of thought, will then be, at least in part, an object of description; and, in consequence, the acquired meaning of the word "man" will result partly from naming by acquaintance and partly from naming by description.

If we turn from the word "man" to the word "meson," we come to a word which is now in the dictionary of the English language but which is a meaningless notation for most individuals who have not looked it up in the dictionary or who have not studied nuclear physics. When they hear the sound, they may not even know that it is the sound of a technical term in that science; for them it may not differ in any way from the sound of a nonsense syllable, such as "trilop." How does the meaningless notation "meson" acquire the referential significance for them that it has for nuclear physicists, or even some meaning remotely approximating that significance?

The only possible answer is that it acquires meaning for the uninitiated through the mediation of verbal descriptions. In fact, since the meson is not an object of perceptual acquaintance for anyone, the notation "meson" must have acquired its significance as a technical term in nuclear physics by being imposed by scientists on an object of thought which they are able to conceive only at the instigation of verbal descriptions. For the nuclear scientist as well as for the layman, the meson is an object of description; and, for both, the use of the initially meaningless notation "meson" as a meaningful common name involves naming by description, not naming by acquaintance.

Question 6. How do the meaningless notations that become syncategorematic words acquire their syntactical significance, and how does that mode of meaning differ from the referential significance of categorematic words or name-words?

We are concerned here with the group of words which have been called particles or syncategorematic words and which we have called linguistic operators, such words as articles ("the" and "a"); prepositions (e.g., "of," "to," "for," "from," etc.); conjunctions and disjunctions (e.g., "and," "either/or," "not both," etc.); and copulas, both positive and negative ("is" and "is not").

I have already pointed out that, unlike categorematic words or name-words having referential significance, such words have only syntactical significance (see Chapter II, Question 4). As we have seen, to say this is to characterize such words in the following manner: (i) they have meaning only as somehow qualifying, modifying, or relating the meanings of other words; (ii) they do not have meaning apart from the syntactical role they play; i.e., the grammatical and logical operations that we use them to perform, or the ways in which we use them to construct phrases and sentences and to formulate propositions. They are secondary, auxiliary, or adjunct words. Categorematic name-words are the primary words of any language, words that have one or more definite or determinate meanings in and of themselves and not as modifiers of or adjuncts to other words.

In answering earlier questions in this chapter, I have confined our attention exclusively to solving the problem of the acquisition of meaning by meaningless notations which become categorematic name-words having referential significance. We must look for a different solution of the problem when we consider meaningless notations which become syncategorematic words or syntactical operators.

How do the meaningless notations that become these secondary, auxiliary, or adjunct words acquire their syntactical significance, if it is not by imposition upon the objects of perception, memory, imagination, and thought? That is one of the questions to be answered here. The other question is: What do such words signify, or what is meant by them, if they do not signify or refer to objects that we are able to apprehend by our acts of perception, memory, imagination, and thought? Because answering the second question will greatly facilitate answering the first, I will begin with it.

At the outset, let us be clear about one negative point: syncategorematic words or linguistic operators certainly do *not* signify or refer to objects of perception, memory, and imagination. But why cannot "and," "of," "the," "therefore" and words of this sort signify objects of thought?

If syncategorematic words signify objects of thought, the objects that they signify are of a very special sort, radically different from all the other objects of conceptual thought—objects which, in respect to the difference under consideration, are comparable to the objects of perception, memory, and imagination. With an understanding of this difference will come an understanding of why it is right to distinguish the referential significance of categorematic words, or words that name objects, from the syntactical significance of syncategorematic words, or linguistic operators.

With very few exceptions to be noted later (see Chapter VII, Question 3), objects of conceptual thought, like objects of perception, memory, and imagination, fall under the categories of real existence, actual or possible; and that is the reason why the words which signify or refer to them are called categorematic. In sharp contrast, the special sort of objects signified by syncategorematic words or linguistic operators are operations of the human mind—either the grammatical operations involved in forming phrases and sentences or the logical operations involved in constructing propositions.

The individual mind is reflexively aware of its own acts, such as its acts of apprehending, judging, and reasoning, as well as of its grammatical and logical operations; and it is on the basis of such reflexive awareness that the mind is able to arrive at a conceptual understanding of these acts and operations. The concepts thus formed should be called reflexive to differentiate them and their objects from all other concepts and conceptual objects. With these points understood, we can say that syncategorematic words signify objects of reflexive thought, those objects being the mind's grammatical and logical operations; whereas, in contradistinction, categorematic words (with exceptions to be noted) signify or refer to objects of perception, memory, and imagination and to those conceptual objects which are *not* objects of reflexive thought.

Another way of making the same point is to say that categorematic words name, signify, or refer to objects that we are able to apprehend, whereas syncategorematic words or linguistic operators signify the grammatical operations that we perform when we construct phrases or sentences and the logical operations that we perform when we construct propositions. It is through our understanding of these operations that we understand the meaning of syncategorematic words. To understand these operations is to understand how syncategorematic words are used, grammatically and logically. Their meaning (or, more precisely, their syntactical significance) derives from an understanding of their use as linguistic operators.

It is easier to see this in the case of logical operations than in the case of grammatical operations. The significance of the word "and" is the logical operation of conjunction; of "either/or," the logical operation of disjunction; of "is not," the logical operation of formulating a negative proposition or a denial. Where we are dealing with the logical syntax of propositions, the significance of the syncategorematic words which are linguistic operators involves not only an understanding of how such words are to be used as operators but also a reflexive awareness of the acts of judgment and of reasoning which lie behind the verbal formulation of propositions and syllogisms. To understand the significance of words of this sort is to be reflexively aware of how one's mind works when it judges or reasons, and expresses its judgments and reasonings in verbally formulated propositions or syllogisms.

Grammatical conventions are less clearly intellectual than logical rules. Nevertheless, our understanding of how to use the definite and the indefinite articles, "the" and "a," involves an understanding of the difference between denoting one particular as distinct from all others and referring to any one of a number of particulars. We use the definite article "the" in constructing phrases which are definite descriptions and which are synonymous with proper names in their existential denotation. We use the indefinite article "a" in constructing phrases which are indefinite descriptions and which are synonymous with common names in their referential significance. The definite and indefinite articles are thus seen to function not only as grammatical operators in phrase-building, but also as logical operators in the construction of definite and indefinite descriptions the existential denotation of which, or their lack of it, affects the truth of the propositions in which these expressions occupy the position of the subject term.

When we come to prepositions—"of," "to," "for," "by," and so forth—which probably form the largest group of syncategorematic words, all we can say is that their syntactical significance consists in our understanding of how to use them to construct phrases that relate one categorematic word to another. Underlying the grammatical relationships are relationships between apprehended objects—relationships of direction, possession, place, time, position, and so forth. Although relations between apprehended objects are themselves objects that we apprehend, prepositions used as linguistic operators do not refer to them. We have categorematic words or phrases at our disposal for that purpose. Prepositions merely perform a grammatical function in phrase-building and their sense—or syntactical significance—derives from our understanding of how to use them for this purpose.

In that last statement lies the answer to the question of how meaningless notations acquire the syntactical significance which turns them into syncategorematic words or syntactical operators: by voluntary imposition on objects of the special sort which has now been defined—the mind's own acts and operations as objects of reflexive thought. This involves an understanding of how to use such words according to the conventions of the language or the rules of logic. I pointed out earlier, in the case of categorematic words, that their referential meaning or designative significance determines their use (see Chapter II, Question 5). The relation of meaning and use is exactly the opposite in the case of syncategorematic words: their use determines their meaning (i.e., their syntactical significance). Here in order to discover the meaning, it is expedient to look for the use.

I am now in a position to make a comprehensive statement concerning the acquisition of meaning by meaningless notations, covering the coming to be of both categorematic and syncategorematic words. For a notation to become or be meaningful, two conditions must be satisfied: (i) it must itself be an object of perception; and (ii) the perception of the notation must be accompanied by an act of understanding, either an understanding of objects (in the case of categorematic words) or a reflexive understanding of the operations of the mind (in the case of syncategorematic words). In the case of categorematic words, the meaningless notation acquires referential significance by imposition on an object understood, whether that object is merely an object of thought or also an object of perception, memory, or imagination. In the case of syncategorematic words, the meaningless notation acquires syntactical significance from an understanding of its use according to grammatical conventions or logical rules, underlying which is an understanding of the operations of the human mind as they affect the employment of language.

I submit that the theory expounded in the course of answering the questions raised in this chapter offers the only tenable solution of the basic problems in the philosophy of language—the problem of how meaning is acquired by meaningless notations and the problem of what is meant by the meaningful words of a language, both categorematic and syncategorematic. I also submit that the solution advanced not only solves those problems, but also solves them in a way that accounts for the use of language as an instrument of communication.

The theory having been expounded, what remains to be undertaken is an examination of its underpinnings and a defense of them. Beyond that, I must deal with the special problems to which the underpinnings give rise as well as the difficulties they engender. These things will be done in the chapters to follow.

Four.
The Underpinnings of the Theory

Preamble

*T*he solution of the problem of meaning, proposed in Chapter III, rests on certain underlying points of theory. Some of these have already been touched on in the course of stating the solution, and now need to be made quite explicit. Some that may not yet have been evident need to be made so.

The basic underpinnings of the theory are its posits—assertions of the existence of theoretical entities or constructs—so called because the theory requires them in order to solve the problem at hand. They may be unobserved, or even unobservable, entities which the theory must postulate in order to account for that which is to be explained; or they may be distinctions and relationships to which the theory must appeal for the same purpose.

The a posteriori procedure that I am following is a familiar one in scientific investigation and should be equally familiar in philosophical thought, though in fact it is much rarer there. It consists in positing whatever is needed to explain the phenomena to be accounted for, and, with proper parsimony, positing nothing beyond what is needed. These posits may be either intimated or evident in the statement already made of the explanatory theory, but the rule of procedure is that all posits should be fully explicit, so that no indispensable theoretical posits remain hidden or concealed. Finally, the posits needed for the purposes of an explanatory theory must themselves be made as reasonable as possible. In addition to justifying them as indispensable theoretical prerequisites, I must attempt to answer whatever questions the consideration of them may raise. I will do that in Chapter V.

I have already touched on these points of a posteriori procedure in the answer to Question 3 of Chapter I, but they are worth reiterating here, especially the point that the theory we have proposed does not involve any prior ontological, epistemological, or psychological commitments. In the course of following the analysis and argument set forth in the preceding chapter, the reader will certainly have noted, and perhaps will even have demurred at, a number of assertions that would appear to have the character of commitments about the acts and processes of cognition, and about the way in which the mind works. That such assertions or commitments were in fact made is conceded, but we are now prepared to show that all of them are posterior rather than prior commitments. They are all posits needed for the development of the explanatory theory which has been proposed, not posits made in advance of or without regard to an attempt to solve the problem of meaning in the philosophy of language.

Attention should be called to one point which has not been previously mentioned. It is a negative point; namely, that the posits required do not involve commitments about the structure or components of reality, about what does or does not really exist, about how the components of reality fall into certain categories of existence, or about how real existents are related to one another. There is one exception to the foregoing statement. I have posited the existence of the human mind as an indispensable factor in the solution of the problem of meaning. That, however, involves us in no commitment to one or another theory of the relation of mind to body, beyond the assertion that mind is at least analytically distinct from body.

IV. Underpinnings of the Theory

In this chapter, I will first enumerate all the posits required; then attempt to answer questions about the character of certain entities that have been posited; and finally deal with distinctions and relationships in the sphere of these posited entities. I will do this in the following order: 1. What posits are required for a solution of the problem of meaning? 2. As compared with really existent things, what mode of existence do subjective ideas have? 3. As compared with things and ideas, what mode of existence do apprehended objects have? 4. What relationships obtain between things and ideas, between ideas and objects, and between objects and things? 5. Does the distinction between three modes of being, appropriate to things, ideas, and objects, call for a distinction between modes of cognition? 6. Is human experience all of one piece, or can it be divided into objective and subjective experience? 7. How does human discourse deal with matters of subjective experience or with what is not experienceable at all?

The answers given to Questions 6 and 7 will not deal with underpinnings of the theory which has been offered as a solution of the basic problem of meaning. They will deal with certain consequences of points made in answer to Questions 1-5, consequences necessitated by a consistently unequivocal use of words.

Question 1. What posits are required for a solution of the problem of meaning?

Let me begin by enumerating them without comment, and follow that with such comments as may be necessary to clarify what is involved in the posits enumerated. In the course of commenting on the posits, I will make some stipulations about terminology that may prove useful in answering subsequent questions.

With regard to considerations of existence, I have posited (i) the existence of mind as at least analytically distinct from body; (ii) the existence of certain acts of the mind, such acts of apprehension as perception, memory, imagination, and conception, as well as acts of judgment and reasoning; (iii) the existence of the products of such acts, particularly the products of the acts of apprehension, all of which I have grouped together under the heading of subjective ideas; and (iv) the existence of the objects apprehended by subjective ideas, as distinct both from the subjective existence of ideas and from the real existence of things. It will be noted that the foregoing posits with regard to existence also involve posits concerning the operations of the human mind.

Not all of the foregoing posits need further elaboration or defence. For example, the answers to Questions 1 and 2 in Chapter III suffice to show why the human mind, its acts, and products are indispensable factors in the solution of the problem of meaning; and also why the acts and products of the mind must be at least analytically distinct from—i.e., not completely reduced to or identified with—brain states and processes. Nor is there any need to explain or defend the distinction between perception and memory, or between memory and imagination. No one acquainted with ordinary human discourse would challenge the statement that we are sometimes engaged in talking to one another about what we are perceiving, sometimes about what we are remembering, and sometimes about what we are imagining. I will deal subsequently with a special problem concerning an object that is perceived by one person, remembered by a second, and imagined by a third; but that there is a difference between perceiving, remembering, and imagining is not likely to be questioned by anyone, nor is it likely to be misunderstood.

The answer to Question 3 in Chapter III also suffices to show why the mind's own subjective ideas cannot be the objects which we apprehend when we perceive, remember, imagine, or think. This, as I have noted, is tantamount to saying that subjective ideas are inapprehensible, uninspectable, and unexperienceable by the individual who uses them as the means or instruments of apprehension, being solely that by which he apprehends whatever it is that he apprehends, but never that which he apprehends. This would be equally true if brain states or processes were the means whereby we apprehend whatever it is that we apprehend: the individual cannot apprehend his own brain states at the same time that he is apprehending that which they serve to make apprehensible. Brain states and processes, however, are not totally inapprehensible. The analytical distinction between mind and body, or between subjective ideas and brain states, rests on the claim that ideas are totally inapprehensible by anyone; whereas brain states, while inapprehensible by the individual whose brain states they are, while they are functioning as his means of apprehension, can be objects of apprehension by neurophysiologists, and under very special circumstances even perhaps by the individual whose brain states they are. I will deal more fully with these matters in my answer to Question 2 when I treat the subjective existence of ideas.

With regard to considerations of cognition, there is one minor epistemological posit and one major psychological posit. The first, the distinction between the acts of apprehending and of judging, has already been adumbrated in Chapter III (see Question 3), where the point was made that the ideas by which we apprehend objects are neither true nor false; our apprehensions are neither correct nor erroneous, though an apprehension may lead to a correct or erroneous judgment—a judgment which is true or false. Only judgments, involving as they do affirmations or denials, must be either true or false.

What must be commented on here is why positing this distinction is necessary. The reason is that without it we cannot distinguish between (i) the referential significance of name-words when their designative meanings are considered and (ii) the existential denotation of such words when they occupy the position of the subject in sentences that are construed as existential propositions. Referential significance involves no concern with truth or falsity; existential denotation, on the contrary, must be considered in the context of questions about the truth or falsity of propositions or judgments. The analysis of existential denotation belongs to logic, not to the philosophy of language. In addition, without the distinction between apprehending and judging, we could not explicate the point that naming is not asserting.

Still within the sphere of cognition, the major psychological posit is the distinction between the kind of objects that can be apprehended by perception, memory, and imagination, on the one hand, and the kind of objects that can be apprehended by conception, understanding, or thought, on the other. This distinction has been touched on earlier, where attention was called to the fact that we never apprehend individuals-as-such, but always particulars, each one of a kind. This, however, is impossible unless we can also apprehend the kinds to which particulars belong. It follows, therefore, that acts of perception, memory, or imagination, by which we apprehend particulars, must be conjoined with acts of conception or understanding, by which we apprehend kinds (see Chapter III, Question 2). In addition, our common experience of human discourse reveals that we often talk about kinds even when we are not apprehending particular instances of them and even when there may be a question whether particular instances of them can be apprehended. Further elaboration of this posited distinction between conceptual and perceptual thought, or between acts of understanding and acts of perception, memory, and imagination, will occur in Chapter VII when we deal with the familiar problem of the universal as it relates to the philosophy of language.

Once again what must be commented on here is why positing this distinction is necessary. The reason is that without it we cannot explain the difference between the referential significance of proper names and definite descriptions, on the one hand, and the referential significance of common names and indefinite descriptions, on the other; nor can we explain the difference between the syntactical significance of the definite article "the" and the syntactical significance of the indefinite article "a" (see Chapter III, Question 6).

What remains to be commented on are posits in the sphere of existence, which involve the threefold distinction of (i) the mode of being that belongs to things that exist independently of the acts of the human mind, (ii) the mode of being that belongs to subjective ideas, and (iii) the mode of being that belongs to the objects that subjective ideas serve to apprehend. These distinctions will be treated in Questions 2 and 3 to follow, and the relationships that obtain among the entities which have these distinct modes of existence will be discussed in Question 4. Here, by way of comment, it is, first of all, necessary to explain why these posited distinctions in modes of existence are necessary for a solution to the problem of meaning; and, after that, it may be useful to point out the special character of these ontological posits and to lay down certain terminological stipulations that I beg the reader to observe and acquiesce in for the purpose of ensuring clarity and precision with regard to the points made in the chapters to follow.

In the solution of the problem of meaning that I have advanced, meaningless notations acquire referential significance through being imposed on objects of perception, memory, imagination, and thought; and reasons were given why neither of the alternative proposals—imposition on really existent things or on subjective ideas—affords a satisfactory solution of the problem. It was also pointed out that that which, as an apprehended object, is the referent or significate of a name-word may be an entity which does not really exist, or which may not have instantiation in reality. In addition, it was pointed out that the ideas by which an individual apprehends objects exist only in his own mind. Their subjective existence is mental. The solution of the problem of meaning, which requires the distinction of objects from both things and ideas, also requires that we posit a mode of existence distinct from the real existence of things and the mental existence of ideas.

This ontological posit of three modes of existence has a very special character. It presupposes nothing about the structure of reality itself or about the nature of its constituents. Even the word "thing," which we have used to designate any really existent entity, is here being used without prejudice to one or another theory about the components of reality—whether they are all events, whether some are continuants having an enduring identity, whether they can be divided into substances and attributes of substances, whether they are all physical bodies or physical forces, and so on.

Reality, as we ordinarily use the term, is that which exists quite apart from the human mind and without any necessary relation to it. Even the relation between reality and the human mind, in which reality is the knowable and the human mind the knower, does not affect the structure or constituents of reality. They are whatever they are whether they are known or not. Subtract mind from the picture and they remain exactly the same. These considerations should enable us to see that the distinct modes of existence, appropriate respectively to ideas and their objects, must be introduced only when the human mind is left in the picture as a cognitive agent.

Of the three modes of existence with which we are concerned, two—the two that are distinct from real (or extramental) existence—must be posited by a theory of meaning that is explanatory of human discourse because the human mind and its acts must be posited in order to explain how meaningless notations become meaningful words. If the human mind and its acts were not necessary factors in the explanation of meaning, it would not be necessary to posit the existence of ideas or the existence of objects as distinct from the existence of things.

In the foregoing statement, three words—"things," "ideas," and "objects"—are obviously employed as critical terms of analysis, each having a very special theoretical import. In our analytical vocabulary, they are never interchangeable, or substitutable one for another. An idea is never a thing or an object; an object, never a thing or an idea; a thing, never an object or an idea. Attention, however, must be called to the fact that, both in ordinary and also in philosophical discourse, these three words are frequently used in other ways—ways that contravene the stipulations I think it necessary to make concerning how I intend to use them.

The words "object" and "thing" are often used interchangeably, as when ordinary men or philosophers speak of this or that physical thing as a physical object. Ideas are said by some philosophers to be objects that we apprehend; and they are said by other philosophers to be objects that have real existence, and they are sometimes regarded as if they were propositions or judgments, as in the expression "the idea that Mars is uninhabited," or in the theory of clear and distinct ideas. Men frequently appear to be engaged in conversation about the ideas they have, as if their subjective ideas were objects of discourse; and the word "idea" is often used, in such phrases as "the idea of freedom" or "the idea of justice," to refer to objects that men are able to think about and discuss with one another, not for the thoughts which each of them may have about such objects.

In view of the prevalence of these contrary and conflicting usages, I find it necessary to stipulate, as plainly as possible, how I shall use these three critical words in the pages that follow. My controlling aim is to use them consistently in a strictly unequivocal fashion—each critical term in one clearly defined sense and only in that sense.

(1) I will use the word "idea" always and only for an individual's perceptions, memories, and imaginations, and conceptions or thoughts—solely the products of the acts of his own mind, and

therefore exclusively his own; I will never use the word "idea" for objects that can be apprehended in any way, referred to by words or talked about, and certainly not for that which can have real existence, i.e., an existence independent of the acts of the human mind.

(2) I will use the word "object" always and only for that which the human mind apprehends by its ideas. I will never use the word for that which really exists independently of the acts of the human mind, or for the feelings of which we are directly aware.

(3) I will use the word "thing" always and only for that which really exists and would exist exactly as it is if the human mind did not exist and were not operative. This stipulation about the use of the word "thing" may be more onerous than the preceding stipulations about the use of "idea" and of "object," because the word "thing" has been so widely used, both in philosophical and in ordinary discourse, to designate any item whatsoever that can be thought about, talked about, or mentioned in any way. I will use the word "entity" in that unrestricted sense for anything that can be thought about, talked about, or mentioned; and as thus used, the word "entity" will not connote one or another mode of existence. An idea is an entity; an object is an entity; a thing is an entity; one and the same entity can be both an object and a thing, but never both an object and an idea or an idea and a thing. I have found it necessary to restrict the word "thing" as the name for one class of entities, those which exist independently of the human mind and of human awareness.

Question 2. As compared with really existent things, what mode of existence do subjective ideas have?

Subjective ideas, as I have repeatedly said, are that by which we apprehend whatever we apprehend, and never that which we apprehend. I have also said that they are the products of certain mental acts—such as perceiving, remembering, imagining, and conceiving or understanding. Before I undertake to answer the question concerning the mode of existence that belongs to the products of these mental acts (i.e., to percepts, memories, images, and concepts), it is necessary to ask a prior question. In view of their being totally inapprehensible, how do we know that ideas exist?

The answer turns on the distinction between judging and apprehending, a distinction to which I have already called attention and to which I will return later in Question 5. There are many objects of thought concerning which we raise questions of existence. The elementary particles posited by the nuclear physicist, for example, are conceptual objects; it is part of the conception of such objects that it is impossible for us to apprehend perceptible instances of them; they are said to be imperceptible by our sense-organs, though traces of their movements can be observed. The fact that nuclear particles and even atoms are imperceptible by us does not preclude our obtaining empirical evidence which can ground an inference as to their real existence.

When the question is raised concerning the existence of elementary particles and when it is answered affirmatively, the following grounds are offered in support of that affirmation: (i) that empirical evidence justifies the inference that such particles exist; and (ii) that they must be posited as theoretical constructs in order to account for the phenomena being studied by the nuclear physicist. On either basis, it would not be improper to say, with certain qualifications of caution, that we know that elementary particles exist, even though no elementary particle is or can ever be an object of perception.

This example of that which is imperceptible and yet also known to exist provides us with a parallel to follow in answering the question about the existence of our inapprehensible subjective ideas. Though we cannot perceive the particular percept by which we apprehend a particular perceptual object, we can conceive what percepts are. We do so when we understand a percept to be the product of the act of perceiving and the means or instrumentality by which we are able to apprehend objects of a certain sort. The word "percept" signifies a conceptual object or object of thought just as the word "ion" or "meson" does. As in the case of "ion" or "meson," so "percept" names a conceptual object; and exactly as in the case of "ion" or "meson," that conceptual object has no particular instances which are objects of perception. In other words, no particular percept is apprehensible by perception, memory, imagination, or thought, even though the class of entities to which particular percepts belong can be apprehended by thought as a conceptual object.

How, then, do we know that the class of entities so conceived is not a null or empty class? How do we know that particular percepts exist? The answer parallels the answer given above to the same question about particular elementary particles. In this case, the empirical evidence that might be offered as a basis for inferring the existence of particular percepts is the reflexive awareness we have of our own acts of perceiving, each singular act being numerically distinct from other singular acts of the same sort. These numerically distinct acts of perceiving sometimes have the same object and sometimes distinct objects; in the latter case, the acts themselves being of the same sort, the only way to account for the difference in their objects is by saying that the products of these acts—the percepts—are different. If two acts of perception which were only numerically distinct also had products (i.e., percepts) that were only numerically distinct, it would be impossible to account for a difference in their objects that was more than a numerical distinction.

In addition to this basis for inferring the existence of a variety of particular percepts, even though none is apprehensible in any way, we can say, as we can say of elementary particles in nuclear physics, that the explanation of the phenomena to be accounted for (in this case, the phenomena of perception) justifies our positing the existence of a variety of particular percepts. We do use words to refer to a wide variety of perceptual objects. If these perceptual objects are that which we not only apprehend but also designate referentially by words, it is necessary to posit that by which we apprehend them. As we have seen, that by which we apprehend a variety of perceptual objects cannot be a number of acts of perception that are only numerically distinct but otherwise essentially the same. Hence it is necessary to posit products of those acts—percepts—with a variety proportionate to the variety of the objects apprehended by acts of perception.

What has just been said about acts of perception and the variety of percepts applies equally to acts of remembering and the variety of memories, acts of imagination and the variety of images, acts of thought and the variety of concepts. Just as in the case of percepts, so also in the case of memories, images, and concepts, we can apprehend, as an object of conceptual thought, the class of entities to which particular memories, images, and concepts belong; but we cannot apprehend *in any way* a particular memory, a particular image, or a particular concept, any more than we can apprehend a particular percept.

I am now prepared to answer the question concerning the mode of existence possessed by subjective ideas. The answer may at first appear to be oversubtle, but I hope that, upon reflection, it will recommend itself as no more complicated than it needs to be. It involves two separate points. (i) On the one hand, if real existence is that mode of existence which is completely independent of individual human minds and their acts, then ideas, as the products of those acts, do not have real existence. Since they depend for their existence on the mental acts of a particular individual or subject, it would seem appropriate to characterize their existence as both subjective and mental. An individual's ideas exist in him and only in him. (ii) On the other hand, if real existence is that mode of existence in which whatever really exists is what it is regardless of whether it is apprehended or even apprehensible, then an individual's subjective ideas can also be said to have real existence as well as subjective existence. Just as a particular human being may really exist regardless of whether he is apprehended by other human beings or known to exist by them, so, too, his mind, its acts, and their products—ideas—may really exist under the same conditions. From that point of view, his mind, its acts, and its ideas do not have subjective existence any more than his body and its aspects, parts, and motions do. But from another point of view, his ideas have exclusively mental existence, as distinct from real existence when that is conceived as existence completely independent of mental acts.

Mention of the human body, its aspects, parts, and motions leads us to recognize the fact that a man's particular complexion exists in him and only in him. In this respect, his complexion does not differ from his ideas, which also exist in him and only in him. On that ground, both his complexion and his ideas might be said to have subjective existence, the one subjective bodily existence, the other subjective mental existence. Since for the purposes of this discussion we are concerned only with the subjective existence of a man's ideas, and not with the subjective existence of his bodily attributes, let us henceforth use the phrase "mental existence" as short for "subjective mental existence." To say that a particular man's ideas have mental existence is to say that they exist in his mind and only in his mind as the products of that mind's activity.

Two other observations should be added to complete this discussion of the mental existence of ideas as the means or instrumentalities of apprehension. A microscope or a telescope is a means or instrumentality of apprehension. While we are using it as an instrument of apprehension, we cannot at the same time make it an object of apprehension; but it can certainly become an object of apprehension for us at some other time when we examine it instead of using it. Ideas differ from microscope, telescopes, or other physical instruments of apprehension in that we can never turn from using them to examining them. They are intrinsically unexaminable or uninspectable, as contradistinguished from all physical instrumentalities of apprehension.

This raises a question about the brain in relation to the mind, or about brain states in relation to ideas. We know that brains and brain states are observable by neurophysiologists, and, through elaborate contrivances, perhaps even by the individual person whose brain or brain state it is. This, by itself, suffices to support the proposition that ideas and brain states are at least analytically distinct, for they differ in at least one important respect; namely, examinability or inspectability. The analytical distinction thus established between mind and brain, or between ideas and brain states, leaves quite open the basic question whether brain states are only the necessary, or also the sufficient, condition for the existence of ideas. Either answer to that question is compatible with a solution of the problem of meaning that posits the mental existence of ideas, and regards them as analytically distinct from brain states because they are intrinsically unexaminable or uninspectable.

Question 3. As compared with things and ideas, what mode of existence do apprehended objects have?

A slight restatement of the question will facilitate answering it. In the reply to the preceding question, we saw that real existence is existence in complete independence of the human mind; and that mental existence is existence in dependence on a particular human mind. That which exists, and is whatever it is quite apart from the mind and its acts, exists in reality; that which exists only as a product of the acts of a particular human mind, exists mentally. We are thus led to ask: What middle ground is there between complete independence of the human mind and dependence on the acts of a particular human mind?

Were there no middle ground or third alternative, it would be difficult to characterize a mode of existence distinct from real existence and mental existence; but there is an alternative and a middle ground. Stated negatively, it consists (i) in not being dependent on the acts of any particular human mind, and in this respect it differs from mental existence; and (ii) in not being independent of the human mind in general, or of all particular minds, and in this respect it differs from real existence. It is a mode of existence that depends on there being some minds at work, but not on the acts of any particular mind. If there were no minds at all in the universe, there would still be things having real existence, but there would be no apprehended objects. If this or that particular mind were not in existence and operative, its subjective ideas would not exist, but there would still be objects apprehended by other minds.

Three men are looking at the moon and talking about it. The moon they are looking at is one and the same really existent thing in the physical universe; and the content of their conversation indicates that it is one and the same perceived object that they are talking about. It is an object for each of them because each has a percept of it. Three men; three percepts; three quite distinct mental existences; but the three percepts are the same in intention; that is, while three in number, they are natural signs having the same significance, and hence the same significate—the moon as object. If that were not so, three men looking at the moon could not have one and the same apprehended object as a common object of reference to talk about.

Continuing with this example, let us now suppose that one of the three men walks away. The really existent moon is totally unaffected; but the same is equally true of the apprehended moon that is the object referred to in the continuing conversation of the other two men. Even if a second of the three men should walk away and the conversation ceased, the moon as a perceived object of the one remaining man would still be unaffected; it would still be an object that he could talk about to a fourth man, should that fourth individual come up a moment later and engage in conversation about it. The fact that the apprehended moon is a common object of discourse for any two men at a given time indicates that it can be a common object of discourse again at a later time for another pair of men. If there were no men at all on earth, the moon would still continue to exist in reality, but there would be no apprehended moon. The moon as a perceptual object depends for its special mode of existence on the operation of one or more minds, but on none in particular.

What this example teaches us holds for any other object that can be a common object of apprehension and of verbal reference for two or more minds. It holds for Hamlet and Julius Caesar, for horses and centaurs, for angels and electrons, for events remembered as well as for events perceived, and for objects of imagination and of thought as well as for objects of perception.

Let us consider another example which involves a remembered object that three men are talking about. The three were some time ago among the pallbearers at the funeral of a mutual friend. They are now discussing the fittings of the casket they carried then. They are in agreement that the fittings were bronze. The casket, as a physical thing, was something that all three of them laid hold of; it was one and the same thing for all three of them. The casket, as an object now being remembered, is also common—one and the same object for all three of them. If, during the funeral, one of them had taken his hands off the casket and walked away, that physical thing would have been considerably affected by his physical removal, whereas the remembered casket would not be at all affected if one of the three men who are engaged in conversation about it were to leave the group and the conversation were then continued by the remaining two.

I have characterized the mode of existence that belongs to apprehended objects, which are also objects of discourse, but I have not yet assigned a name to it. In view of the fact that ideas are natural signs which signify, refer to, or intend objects as their natural referents or significates, it would seem appropriate to speak of the mode of existence possessed by objects as *intentional* existence. What was said earlier about subjective ideas (that they *are* meanings; that their very nature *is* to signify) can now be restated by saying that ideas are intentions of the mind. Their intentionality consists in their having significates or objects. Objects, as intended or signified, have intentional existence.

Let me now summarize the threefold distinction in modes of existence which has emerged from the answers given to Questions 2 and 3. I. *Real* existence (i.e., the existence possessed by things) is that mode of being which is totally independent of mind—independent of mind in general and of any particular mind. II. *Mental* existence (i.e., the existence possessed by subjective ideas) is that mode of being which is totally dependent on the acts of a particular mind. III. *Intentional* existence (i.e., the existence possessed by apprehended objects or objects of discourse) is that mode of being which is dependent on mind in general—dependent on the acts of some particular minds, but not dependent on the acts of any one particular mind.

The realm of real existence includes things that are apprehensible or knowable but that are not in fact apprehended or known. The realm of intentional existence includes entities that exist as objects but not as things, as well as entities that have both real and intentional existence; that is, exist both as things and as objects (e.g., the moon looked at and perceived; the casket carried and remembered). It may, in addition, include entities that exist only as objects and never as things; that is, entities that have intentional existence but cannot have real existence.

In the foregoing statement, I have used the word "entity" as a completely neutral term, prescinding from the distinction between real and intentional existence. It would be incorrect and thoroughly misleading to speak of a thing which is also an object, or of an object which is also a thing. That which is a thing is never, as such, an object; that which is an object is never, as such, a thing; but one and the same entity—the moon or the casket in the examples we considered—can be both a thing looked at or carried and also an object perceived or remembered. One and the same entity can have both real and intentional existence; or it may have one or the other mode of existence but not both. Mental existence has been omitted from this discussion because entities that have either real or intentional existence, or both, do not have mental existence at all. The moon or the casket, which exists as a thing and as an object, does not exist as a subjective idea, though the perception of the moon or the memory of the casket is that which confers intentional existence on an entity which also has or had real existence.

The same point can be stated in another way. We can define a thing as an entity which, in order to be a thing, must have real existence and may or may not have intentional existence; and we can define an object as an entity which, in order to be an object, must have intentional existence and may or may not have real existence. Still another way of stating the point is as follows. The thing-as-such, having real existence, is the thing as apprehensible. The thing-as-apprehended is an object that has intentional existence. The thing-as-such and the thing-as-apprehended are one and the same entity having two modes of existence. Since an object, having intentional existence, depends for its existence on acts of the human mind, though not upon the acts of any one particular mind, objects having intentional existence may be entities that do not have real existence as well, though they may have real existence if the objects happen to be things-as-apprehended.

The crucial importance of the point just made in a number of ways lies in the emphatic denial that apprehended objects are representations (copies, counterparts, or resemblances) of things, even when they put us into a cognitive relation to things that really exist. Neither subjective ideas nor their objects are in any way representations of reality. I shall elaborate on this denial in Question 4 to follow. Here let me conclude by stressing once more the indispensability of this threefold distinction in modes of being for a solution of the problem of meaning that accounts for the use of language as an instrument of communication.

If a full and adequate description of the world were limited to real and mental existences, there would be no common objects of reference for human discourse and no referentially significant words. A world without minds would not only be a world without mental, as opposed to physical, existences; it would also be a world without objects—without entities having intentional existence, whether or not they also have real existence. Referentially significant words cannot name that which is totally inapprehensible (subjective ideas); nor can they name that which in fact is not apprehended (things-as-such). Hence there is nothing left for them to name but apprehended or experienced objects.

If words were to name percepts or concepts (waiving for the moment the utter impossibility of naming the inapprehensible), no communication among men would be possible through the use of name-words, for what would thus be named would be ideas which are wholly subjective or private and cannot be terms of reference for two or more individuals. Furthermore, if words could name only perceptual objects that are entities which also have real existence, most of human discourse would be unintelligible. It would be about nothing at all, for without the intentional existence of conceptual objects, which may or may not have instantiation in reality, the common names of any language would have no referential significance whatsoever. They would be either meaningless notations, or if they had meaning, it would be nonreferential, in which case such words would only appear to be names, whereas in fact they would have to function in some other way.

Question 4. What relationships obtain between things and ideas, between ideas and objects, and between objects and things?

Except for works of art, which are products of human work involving the action of both mind and body, things are not in any way caused by ideas or objects. Things are, however, at least partly the cause of our having some of our ideas—our perceptions and their residues in memory and imagination. The important fact about perception is the sensory input which is its core, overlaid by the products of memory, imagination, and thought. Herein lies the difference between perceiving and hallucinating: there is no sensory input in the latter.

For our purposes, there is no need to explain this by an elaborate account of the ways in which things physically impinge upon our bodily sense-organs and set up trains of neurophysiological events that result in brain states which underlie the mind's acts of perception and subsequent acts of memory or imagination. Nor, for our purposes, is there any need to consider various theories of how concepts are caused, beyond saying that they are not caused by the physical impingement of things on bodily sense-organs in the same way that percepts are caused.

Suffice it to add that the formation of concepts depends on prior acts of perception, memory, and imagination, though concept-formation can never be totally resolved into these acts. Without some perceptual experience and without some memories and imagination, we would not be able to form any concepts at all; but once we have a certain reservoir of concepts at our disposal, we are able to form additional concepts without direct reliance upon perceptual experience or its residues. If that were not the case, we could not form the concepts that enable us to apprehend objects which have no perceptual instances, or of which perceptual instances are impossible.

Ideas, whether or not they are directly caused by things, function as the causes productive of objects. There can be things which, for one reason or another, do not cause ideas in us. There can be ideas which are not directly caused by things. But there cannot be objects which are not caused by ideas. This point merely repeats what has been said before in other terms. Ideas being that by which we apprehend that which we do apprehend, they necessarily function as the causes productive of the objects of our apprehension. The productive causality of ideas is their intentionality—the fact that, by their very nature and being, they signify. To say that ideas, as mental existences, have intentionality is, therefore, to say that they have the power to produce objects; and to say that the objects produced by our ideas have intentional existence is to say that their being consists in their being intended or signified by ideas.

The power of the mind, through having ideas, to make objects for itself is threefold. (i) It is a power to make objects of entities that also really exist, or of classes of entities that have instantiation in reality. (ii) It is a power to make objects of entities that can really exist but do not, or of classes of entities that can have instantiation in reality but do not.

(iii) It is a power to make objects of entities that cannot really exist, or of classes of entities that cannot have instances in the world of really existing things.

So much, then, for the relation between things and ideas, on the one hand, and for the relation between ideas and objects, on the other. What about the relation between objects and things? In our reply to Question 3, I have called attention to the point that the objects of our apprehension are *not* representations of things, even when apprehended objects are elements that enter into our knowledge of things—our judgments concerning what really does or does not exist, or concerning the characteristics of really existing things or their relationships to one another.

Throughout modern thought, it has been said again and again that the objects we apprehend (whether they are identified with our subjective ideas or distinguished from them) represent or somehow stand for the realities concerning which we strive to achieve knowledge. This notion of representation or standing for would appear to convert the objects we apprehend into signs of the really existing things that we do not apprehend. This cannot be the case, however. When X, whatever it is, is a sign of Y, it somehow functions to make Y, something other than itself, present. But when apprehended objects are said to represent or stand for unapprehended things, they do not and cannot make the latter present in place of themselves. Quite the contrary: far from making that which they represent present, they would bar the way to its being present; they would function as surrogates for, not as signs of, that which they represent.

To regard apprehended objects (whether they are identified with our subjective ideas or distinguished from them) as representations—copies, counterparts, resemblances—of reality is a fatal error, from which modern philosophy has suffered from its beginning to the present day. The root of the error lies in neglect or ignorance of the intentional mode of existence that belongs to objects apprehended by the mind. The error can, therefore, be avoided by a precise understanding of the relation between intentionally existing objects and really existing things; to wit, that one and the same entity can have both modes of existence. Since things-as-such and the objects we apprehend have distinct modes of existence (real and intentional), how can we avoid regarding them as two, and the latter as the representation of the former? The answer, once again, is that one and the same entity can be (i) a thing-as-such and, as such, also apprehensible, and (ii) a thing-as-apprehended and, as such, also an object.

What has just been said applies solely to perceptible physical things and perceived objects. It is only in the case of the perceived object and the perceptible thing that we are concerned with their being numerically two and yet somehow one—partly, not completely, identical. Their partial identification is initially accomplished by acknowledging that one and the same entity can have two modes of existence—real existence as a thing and intentional existence as an object. More remains to be said on this subject, to which we will return in Chapter V, Question 2.

Question 5. Does the distinction between three modes of being, appropriate to things, ideas, and objects, call for a distinction between modes of cognition?

I have already touched on the distinction between apprehending and judging as cognitive acts of the mind (see Chapter III, Question 3). This distinction, at first glance, appears to correspond to the distinction between objects having intentional existence and things having real existence; but, upon further examination, the actual state of affairs is somewhat more complicated.

The act of apprehending, which involves no assertions or claims of truth, is always and only an apprehension of objects. Our apprehensions of them, whether perceptual or conceptual, are neither true nor false.

I have called the act of apprehending the first act of the mind because the objects apprehended enter as elements into all subsequent cognitive acts. These subsequent acts are all acts of judging, but some of the judgments made may be immediate judgments, not based on reasoning or inference, and some may be mediated judgments based on reasoning or inference. These subsequent acts of judgment always involve assertions about the objects that we apprehend; and as such they also involve claims concerning the truth of what is asserted.

The judgments of the mind, whether immediate or mediated, can be divided into two groups. (i) They may be existential judgments; that is, they may consist of assertions to the effect that one or another apprehended object is also an entity that does or does not really exist; or, if the object in question is a conceptual object, the existential judgment may take the form of asserting that the object is a class of entities which does or does not have perceptual instances, or instantiation in reality; or even that it is a class of entities which can or cannot have perceptual instances, or instantiation in reality. They may also consist of statements about the characteristics of really existent things or about the ways in which they are related. The truth or falsity of all such assertions lies in their agreement or nonagreement with reality—with what does or does not, can or cannot, really exist. Such truths are often called descriptive truths or truths about matters of fact and real existence. If the judgment asserts that that which is, is, or that that which is not, is not, its claim to being true is valid; and when that is the case, our judgments are the means whereby we have knowledge of reality—the realm of real existences. Just as ideas are that by which we apprehend, not that which we apprehend, so judgments are that by which we know, not that which we know.

(ii) The second group of judgments is characterized as being nonexistential. They assert nothing about what really exists or does not exist, or about what can and cannot exist or be instantiated in reality. Instead, they consist of assertions about the characteristics of certain objects or about their relation to other objects. The truth or falsity of such assertions cannot lie in their correspondence or noncorrespondence with what really exists; rather it must be entirely based on criteria of consistency or coherence within a whole set of statements about the characteristics of apprehended objects or about their relation to one another. In some few cases, as striking as they are rare, the truth of such assertions may be seen at once in the fact that they are the opposites of statements that are self-contradictory.

In the light of the foregoing analysis, the act of judgment, giving rise to assertions that may be either true or false, would appear sometimes to give us knowledge about things as they really exist, and sometimes knowledge about apprehended objects. It does the former when our judgments are existential; the latter, when they are not existential. Mathematical truths fall into the latter group and so do what are sometimes called truths of understanding, in contradistinction to truths about matters of fact or real existence.

What about subjective ideas in the realm of mental existence? They are totally inapprehensible as objects. Can we, then, in any sense of the term, have knowledge about them? The answer is obviously affirmative, at least to the extent that we have knowledge, by inference, that subjective ideas exist (see reply to Question 2). Beyond that, we can have knowledge of the characteristics of the whole class of entities which are subjective ideas, the class itself being an object of conceptual thought. We know, for example, that subjective ideas as mental existences are totally inapprehensible; we know that they are productive of the objects which are their natural significates or referents; and so on. These are all judgments of a nonexistential type, i.e., judgments about the characteristics or properties of a certain class of entities, in this case entities that have only mental existence.

Question 6. Is human experience all of one piece, or can it be divided into objective and subjective experience?

Objective experience comprises the experience of all the objects that we apprehend, whether they are objects of perception, memory, imagination, or thought. It is an experience of objects that either are or can be common to two or more minds, and so can be regarded as public, not private.

If whatever we apprehend is an object, and if all objects are public, how can there be any subjective or private experience—experience that exclusively belongs to one individual and one individual alone?

To answer this question, we must go outside the sphere of the mind's cognitive activites in apprehending objects and in knowing whatever is to be known. We must turn to the sphere of the affects and emotions, such as our feelings of pleasure and pain, hunger and thirst, fear and anger. As I have used the word "ideas" to cover percepts, memories, images, and concepts, so let me now use "bodily feelings" for the variety of affects and emotions. Having such bodily feelings is certainly part of human experience, but it is distinctly different from the objective experience that results from the apprehension of objects. An individual's experience of his own bodily feelings cannot be shared by anyone else; it is exclusively his own; it is, therefore, private, not public, experience.

Let me digress for a moment on the distinction between the public and the private. In the sphere of action, things having real existence are public when they are shared in any way by two or more individuals, or at least have the capability of being shared. The rope that you and I are pulling together, the table that you and I are sitting at, the picture that we are both looking at—these things are public. In the sphere of action, any thing that really exists is, in principle at least, public, though every thing may not in fact be actually public. In the sphere of cognition, all the objects of our apprehension are similarly public in principle: each of them can be an object of apprehension for two or more minds, even though every one of them may not in fact be actually public. Over against (i) the public sphere of action, consisting of the really existent things that we can act together on, and (ii) the public sphere of cognition, consisting of the intentionally existing objects that can be the common objects of our apprehension and discourse, there is (iii) the private sphere of each individual's bodily feelings, the sphere of his subjective experience, exclusively his own; and (iv) the equally private sphere of each individual's reflexive awareness of the acts of his own mind as they are occurring.

There would be no difficulty in understanding this fourfold distinction were it not for the fact that colloquial speech frequently uses the words "feel" and "feeling" as if they referred to acts of cognition. We are accustomed to saying "I feel that such and such is the case" or "I have the feeling that this is so," using these words as if they were substitutes for "opine," "believe," "think," and even "guess," all words that fall short of the full force of "know." If we eliminate all such expressions as colloquial inaccuracies of speech, we are left with statements to the effect "I feel hungry" or "I feel a pain in my thumb." Just as "I feel that such and such is the case" appears to be a statement of knowledge, so "I feel hungry" or "I feel a pain in my thumb" appears to be a statement of apprehension, comparable to the statements "I perceive the moon" or "I remember last night's sunset." If that were the case, then the bodily feeling of hunger or pain would be an object of apprehension, and all experience would be of one piece. It would be entirely objective; there would be no subjective or private experiences which belong to a single individual and cannot be shared by him with anyone else.

This supposition is obviously contrary to fact. I must, therefore, try to make the denial of it as explicit as possible. Feelings are neither cognitive acts nor are they objects of apprehension. We apprehend nothing when we feel; the experience of feelings does not involve us in apprehending anything. What is experienceable consists of (i) the objects that we *apprehend,* (ii) the feelings that we *have,* and, as we pointed out earlier, (iii) the acts of our own minds, of which each of us is *reflexively aware* at the time of their occurrence. Having a bodily feeling does not involve an act of apprehension, though in a broad sense of the term "awareness," which includes more than apprehension, to have a feeling is to be aware of it.

Because what I am trying to say here runs so contrary to ordinary speech and to an uncritical acceptance of its implications, let me repeat the point once more. We do not apprehend feelings of pain or hunger; we have them directly as elements of subjective experience. Familiar expressions are available to reinforce this point. Instead of saying "I feel a pain in my thumb," we could say "I have a thumbache," just as we say "I have a toothache" instead of saying "I feel a pain in my tooth." Similarly, one could say "I have hunger" or "I have anger" instead of "I feel hungry" or "I feel angry."

Just as I observed earlier the importance of not using the words "apprehend" and "judge" interchangeably, so here I am calling attention to the importance of not using the words "apprehend" and "feel" interchangeably. The following statement summarizes the fourfold distinction which should be observed: (i) we *apprehend* objects; (ii) we *have* bodily feelings of which we are aware and which constitute one type of subjective experience; (iii) each of us is *reflexively aware* of the acts of his own mind, and this awareness constitutes another type of subjective experience; and (iv) we *know* that such and such is the case in the realm of real existences, or that such and such are the characteristics and relationships of the objects we have apprehended.

One consequence of the point being made is the recognition of a sharp division between the sphere of bodily feelings and the sphere of ideas. To say that we have, but do not apprehend, the feelings that are elements of our subjective experience is to say that we have no ideas of them. Since a particular bodily feeling which we experience is not apprehended by us as an object, there is no need for us to have an idea of it. This, of course, does not preclude our having a concept of the class of entities to which all bodily feelings belong. Bodily feelings as a class can be an object of thought; if that were not the case, we could not be carrying on this discussion of them and claiming truth for the statement that no particular bodily feeling experienced by us is ever an object that we apprehend.

For the reader who is puzzled by the foregoing discussion because it departs from generally accepted notions and common usage, a word of further explanation may be helpful. Writers are not privileged to legislate about how words should be used, but it is their privilege to adopt a policy of using their critical terms unequivocally and in a consistent fashion. That is the policy I have followed in the writing of this book. It is precisely the effort to adhere to a strictly unequivocal use of words (especially those words which express the critical terms in this analysis and argument) which has necessitated the troublesome or disturbing departures from prevalent notions and ordinary speech.

The following points have been central to this analysis and argument: (i) acts of apprehending produce ideas; (ii) ideas produce objects; (iii) objects either are or can be commonly present to the minds of two or more persons. In the light of these points, it inescapably follows that since the toothache felt by me at this moment cannot be felt by anyone else, it is not an object; hence there can be no idea of it; hence there can be no apprehension of it. However, it does not follow from what has just been said that I am not directly aware of my toothache, or that I cannot have an idea (i.e., a concept) about toothaches in general, in consequence of which that kind of pain can be a conceptual object, common to two or more persons, an object which they can refer to and discuss at a time when none of them is feeling the pain of a toothache.

What has just been said applies to an individual's reflexive awareness of the acts of his own mind as they are occurring. He and he alone can be aware of them; hence they—the particular acts occurring in a particular person's mind at a particular time—are not objects, there can be no idea of them, and they are inapprehensible. Yet, because each of us is reflexively aware of the acts of his own mind, we can form ideas (i.e., concepts) concerning mental acts in general, and this or that type of mental act can become a conceptual object, capable of being apprehended and discussed by two or more persons.

Finally, it is necessary to call attention to the use of the word "subjective" in two distinct contexts. I have used it as an adjective descriptive (i) of the mental existences which are ideas and (ii) of the private experiences we have when we have bodily feelings. What is common to these two uses of the word is its negation of the objective in both cases. Ideas are never objects of apprehension; nor are bodily feelings. But though neither are objects of apprehension, subjective bodily feelings are experienceable as subjective ideas are not. We are thus confronted with the following threefold distinction: (i) the realm of the totally inexperienceable—subjective ideas; (ii) the realm of private or subjective experience—the bodily feelings we have but do not apprehend as well as the mental acts of which each of us is reflexively aware; and (iii) the realm of public or objective experience—the apprehended objects of perception, memory, imagination, and thought.

Question 7. How does human discourse deal with matters of subjective experience or with what is not experienceable at all?

The threefold distinction which we confronted at the end of the reply to the preceding question raises a special problem concerning the referential significance of the words we use when we appear to be discussing either matters that are not experienceable at all or are elements of subjective experience.

Let us begin by considering an individual's subjective experience of pain or hunger. The pain or hunger which he has is experienceable by him alone. How, then, can he talk about it with someone else, as he undoubtedly does when he complains to his dentist about his toothache or to his wife about the lateness of dinner? If the communicative use of language in conversation involves references to common objects of discourse, an individual's remarks about the pain or hunger he is having would appear to be a noncommunicative use of language.

In attempting to solve this problem, the first point to make is one that has been already noted. There is no difficulty in talking about hunger in general or pain in general. The words "pain" and "hunger" name conceptual objects—each a class of particulars, conceived in a certain way. At the level of conceptual thought, we understand what pain is and how it differs from pleasure; we understand what hunger is and how it differs from thirst or anger. These universal objects of conceptual apprehension do not differ from any other universal objects that we are able to apprehend conceptually, such as justice or freedom, electron or angel, and even percept or concept. The fact that particular percepts and concepts are totally inapprehensible does not preclude our conceptual apprehension of the class of entities to which all particular percepts or all particular concepts belong. Similarly, the fact that particular pains or hungers are subjective experiences does not preclude pain in general and hunger in general from being conceptual objects, i.e., conceptually apprehended classes of entities to which all particular pains and all particular hungers belong. This being so, the use of the common names "pain" and "hunger" with referential significance is exactly the same as the use of the common names "electron" and "angel," or the common names "percept" and "concept."

However, the person who talks to the dentist about the toothache he is having does not wish to engage in a discussion of pain in general, or even of toothaches in general. He is trying to tell his dentist about the particular toothache he is having at the moment—in which tooth it is, what it feels like, how intense the pain is, and so on. Since the words he uses must be referring to a purely subjective experience that he is having and that the dentist cannot share, is he communicating? If so, how?

That the person in his chair has a toothache is something that the dentist can know with a fair measure of probability, either by believing the patient's testimony to that effect, or by inference from the patient's behavior, his facial expression, his moans and groans. The dentist, however, cannot apprehend the patient's toothache, for it is not a perceptual object, either for him or for the patient. What, then, does he have in mind when he listens to the patient talk about the toothache he is having? One answer to that question is that all he can have in mind is his understanding or conception of toothaches in general, by which he apprehends the universal object or class of entities to which all particular toothaches belong. Anything beyond that? It could only be the dentist's recollection of a toothache that he himself once had. The bodily feeling of the prior toothache cannot be an object of the dentist's memory, any more than the present toothache of the patient is an object of perception. To say that the dentist recollects a prior toothache is, therefore, to say that a prior subjective experience is now somehow reinstated. But how can that be the case? If the dentist's teeth are not now aching, he cannot now be having the subjective experience of toothache. This does not preclude his remembering having had a toothache at some previous time, though he cannot remember the toothache that he had; nor does it preclude his asserting, as a matter of knowledge, that that prior toothache actually occurred on a certain day and lasted for a certain time.

If, then, it is impossible, as we maintain, to reinstate in the present bodily feelings subjectively experienced at some previous time, the conversation between the patient and the dentist is effectively communicative only at the conceptual level of objective experience, and not at all on the plane of subjective experience. What has just been said applies equally to all the elements of subjective experience—to other particular felt pains as well as toothaches, to particular felt pleasures, to particular bodily feelings of hunger, anger, fear, and so on.

This can all be summed up by saying that subjective experiences are, as such or in their particularity, not communicable. When we appear to be engaged in conversation about them, as, for example, in a patient's talk to his dentist about the toothache he is having, that appearance is deceptive. The conversation is communicative only at the level of the universal, where there are common conceptual objects to which common names can refer; but it is not communicative at the level of the particular, where the bodily feeling is subjectively experienced by only one of the two persons involved.

If an individual's own bodily feelings cannot be the subjects of communicative discourse, it must follow, a fortiori, that language cannot be used communicatively to discuss the particular ideas that an individual has in his own mind. Bodily feelings are elements of subjective or private experience and it is this which excludes them from the sphere of matters that can be publicly discussed. Subjective ideas are totally inexperienceable, and so they are even further removed from the sphere of communicative discourse.

When individuals appear to talk to one another about their ideas of this or that, what in fact they must be doing is talking about the objects of these ideas. Three men looking at the moon are not talking about the numerically distinct percepts that the three of them have, but rather about the one moon which is the common object of their perceptual apprehension; similarly, the three men who remember the fittings on the casket which they helped to carry as pallbearers are not talking about their numerically distinct memories, but about the one object that they all remember.

Five.
Two Difficult Questions

Preamble

*I*n Chapter III, I presented a theory of language that I regard as the only tenable solution of the basic problem of meaning—the only solution of that problem which accounts for the use of language as an instrument of communication. In Chapter IV, I attempted to state as explicitly as possible the underpinnings of that theory, none of them prior philosophical commitments, but rather all of them implicit in the development of the theory itself. These underpinnings included a certain number of posits which needed no other justification than their being required by the theory, such as the posited existence of the human mind as at least analytically distinct from the human body, the mental existence of subjective ideas, the intentional existence of the objects of these ideas, the distinction between the intentional existence of objects and the real existence of things, and so on.

Just as the underlying theoretical points discussed in Chapter IV were implicit in the theory which we presented in Chapter III, so we must now turn to two problems that may have been discernible as implicit in our statement of the posits expounded in Chapter IV. These two problems must now be made explicit; and I must confess, in advance of my attempt to deal with them in this chapter, that I regard them as extremely thorny problems, involving difficulties that I am not sure can be completely overcome.

The problems to be faced are stated in the following questions: 1. How can two or more numerically distinct ideas be the means whereby one and the same object is apprehended? 2. How is a perceptual object related to the really existing thing which causes our perception of that object?

Question 1. How can two or more numerically distinct ideas be the means whereby one and the same object is apprehended?

It is important at the beginning to reaffirm the proposition that gives rise to this problem. The theory we have presented holds steadfastly to the proposition that two or more men are able to converse about one and the same object, an object which they apprehend in common and to which their name-words refer. That proposition, in fact, is the theory's point of departure. With that as an unquestioned given, the theory then undertakes to account for the communicative use of language by what it says concerning the role of subjective ideas as the means by which objects are apprehended, and by what it says concerning the role of objects as the significates or referents of name-words, words which acquired their referential significance by being voluntarily imposed upon the objects of perception, memory, imagination, and thought.

The theory, however, also asserts that the ideas that each man has exist only in his own mind. Hence when two men appear to be talking about one and the same object which they both apprehend, each of them must have an idea by which he apprehends that object, an idea which is numerically distinct from the idea in the mind of the other man. If one of the men were to cease to be, the idea which exists only in his own mind would also cease to be; but its ceasing to be would leave totally unaffected the idea existing in the mind of the other man.

This being so, it is certainly reasonable—more than that, obligatory—to ask how two numerically distinct ideas can be the means by which one and the same object is apprehended. Since the ideas are intrinsically inapprehensible, i.e., unexaminable or uninspectable, we cannot answer the question by examining the ideas themselves; nor can we answer it by assuring ourselves in a variety of ways that the two men are in fact talking about one and the same object. When we do examine instances of human discourse in which men appear to be talking about one and the same object, we find that what appears to be the case is not always actually in fact the case. Sometimes, the course of a critically conducted and sustained conversation will reveal that the participants in it are operating with different ideas and so have different objects in mind, objects that overlap in certain respects but are distinct in others. On the other hand, the steps in a conversation which attempt to check the identity of the object being discussed will sometimes confirm beyond reasonable doubt that the two men are in fact using words to refer to one and the same object, an object that is commonly apprehended by both of them.

This leads us to a restatement of the problem to be solved. The task is not to show that two men, having numerically distinct ideas, are necessarily referring to one and the same object when their use of words suggests that they are talking about an object common to them both. Rather, the task is to show how it can ever be possible for a conversation about one and the same object to take place, in view of the fact that the persons engaged in discourse necessarily have numerically distinct ideas by which they apprehend the object they appear to be discussing.

A first approximation to a solution of the problem is as follows. The plurality of ideas, when two or more men are engaged in conversation, is an existential plurality which may be, but is not necessarily, combined with a unity of intention. Your idea and my idea, by which we apprehend a certain object, can be two in number existentially, even though they are identical in intention, each being an idea that functions as a means of apprehending the object in question.

When two men successively utter the same word, the fact that the two utterances are numerically distinct does not prevent the sound they have uttered from being the same word; nor does it prevent that word from having the same referential significance. The case of two numerically distinct ideas would appear to be similar. Though they are numerically distinct, they can be the same idea in intention, just as the twice-uttered word can be the same word and have the same meaning. There is, in short, nothing intrinsically impossible about there being in the minds of each of two men an idea that, functioning as a natural sign, has the same natural significate or referent. Each man has a numerically distinct instance of the same idea, an idea that is the same precisely because what it signifies or intends is the same, namely, the object which it is the means of apprehending. Hence we seem able to reach the conclusion that when the idea in the mind of one person is only numerically distinct from the idea in the mind of another, and identical in all other respects, the two ideas can be the means whereby the two men apprehend one and the same object.

A rough physical analogy may help to illustrate what has just been said. From the negative of a motion-picture film, two prints can be made. If the prints are properly made, they will be numerically distinct but identical in all other respects. If these two prints are then placed in two projectors, the projectors can be so focussed that they throw perfectly overlapping images on the screen; in effect, one image projected from two films. Alternatively, images might be projected from the two films on screens placed side by side, and the most careful observation of them would not be able to discern any difference between them, other than the fact that they are two.

The identity of an object being discussed by two men, each with his own idea as a means of apprehending it, is established by the discovery of no discernible difference between the object that one man is apprehending and the object apprehended by the other. There are two numerically distinct ideas at work here, just as there are two films running in the two projectors; but just as there is only one set of projected images on the screen, or two sets that are different only numerically, so there is only one object to which the two men are referring; or if there are two objects, they are different only numerically and in no other respect.

If someone were to ask why it is that two ideas can have one object, but one idea cannot have two objects, the answer should be like the answer one would give if asked why two children can have one father, but one child cannot have two fathers. In the case of children and fathers, the fact that a father can have many children, but a child cannot have more than one father, is grounded in the very nature of the procreative relation. So, too, in the case of ideas and objects, the fact that one and the same object can be apprehended by many numerically distinct ideas, but one idea cannot be the means of apprehending more than one object, is grounded in the very nature of the cognitive relation which exists between an idea as that by which an object is apprehended and an object as that which is apprehended by an idea.

One point of perplexity remains to challenge the solution thus far offered. In my reply to Question 4 in Chapter IV, I said that ideas, which are themselves products of the mind's activity, produce the objects that we apprehend. Without the act of perceiving, and the percept thus produced, there would be no perceptual object; without the act of understanding, and the concept thus produced, there would be no conceptual object; and so on. Considering the causal relation between an idea and the object it produces, we are compelled to say that, if two numerically distinct ideas can be the means by which two men apprehend one and the same object, it must follow that two numerically distinct causes can be productive of one and the same effect.

It is a generally accepted view that this cannot happen in the physical world. In the realm of real existences, the operation of numerically distinct causes would necessarily result in the production of numerically distinct effects. If two causes were only numerically distinct, and identical in all other respects (e.g., the striking of two matches), the two effects (e.g., two flames) might be only numerically distinct, while identical in all other respects, but they would, nevertheless, be at least numerically distinct. How, then, can we say that two ideas are productive of one and the same effect—one apprehended object?

Two answers suggest themselves, the first less satisfactory than the second. If one were to concede that, in the sphere of cognition, causality operates exactly as it does in the realm of physical things, one would be led to the conclusion that when each of two men has an idea that is only numerically distinct from the idea in the mind of the other, the objects causally produced by those ideas must also be numerically distinct. To this, we must add that if they are distinct only numerically, and different in no other discernible respect, then their numerical twoness can be overlooked, for they have the identity of indiscernibles in all other respects. The two men have one object before them.

It is, however, not necessary to make the concession indicated. Apprehended objects are entities that exist intentionally. They are not physical entities possessing real existence. The difference between real and intentional existence, and with it, perhaps, the difference between the mode of existence that is appropriate to physical things or events and the mode of existence that is appropriate to apprehended objects, may explain why, in the realm of intentionally existing objects, one and the same object may be the single effect produced by the causal operation of numerically distinct ideas, whereas in the realm of really existing things, that can never be the case (i.e., a single effect cannot be produced by the operation of numerically distinct causes).

Fully to understand the force of what has just been said requires an understanding of the role of matter in the determination of the numerical diversity of two physical things that are two only in number or in space-time, and identical in all other respects. If one could fully understand how matter is the principle of individuation, causing two physical things which are otherwise identical to be distinct in number or in space-time, one might then also fully understand why individuation does not take place in the case of objects which do not have physical existence and do not involve matter.

Stated another way, if two objects were identical in all respects except number, there would be nothing to individuate them and make them two in number. Hence two numerically distinct ideas which are identical in intention can be the means of apprehending one and the same object, even though that one object is causally produced by two numerically distinct ideas. The numerical diversity of the ideas results from the numerical diversity of the persons in whose minds they are; but since the object apprehended by the two minds does not exist in the two minds that apprehend it, the twoness of the minds does not result in a numerical diversification of the object apprehended. Nor can any other factor be thought of which might result in such diversification.

This is as far as I can carry the solution of the problem we have been confronting. That solution calls attention to a number of points which deserve consideration; it overcomes certain difficulties while, at the same time, engendering others. It succeeds in solving the problem only to the extent that one is able to understand matters that lie at the very heart of the problem upon which the solution rests, such as, for example, the source or root of numerical diversification.

Question 2. How is the perceptual object related to the really existing thing which causes our perception of that object?

The question applies only to the object of perception, and not to any other objects of apprehension—objects of memory, imagination, and thought. It is only in the case of perception that we have the pervasive and almost incorrigible impression that what we are perceiving is a really existent thing and not an object having intentional existence. Only in this one type of apprehension, do we apply the distinction between the apprehensible and the apprehended to things: we speak of things that we are not now perceiving as perceptible, and this leads us to speak of things as perceived when the perception of them occurs. We then tend to identify the thing-as-perceived with the perceptual object, though the thing, either as perceptible or as perceived, exists in reality and the perceptual object exists only intentionally. The sharp distinction between things and objects seems to vanish in the case of perception, and with it also the equally sharp distinction between apprehending and knowing; for if in perception we are apprehending things, not just objects, then perception would appear to be an act of judgment involving, at least implicitly, an existential assertion.

We are thus brought face to face with a number of difficulties inherent in the theory that has been expounded in the preceding chapters. They arise as a series of apparent exceptions to important points of theory previously stated as if they were without exception. These embarrassments will be removed only to the extent that I can succeed in showing that these exceptions are more apparent than real.

Let me begin by facing the question exactly in the terms in which it has been posed. It asks about the relationship between the perceptual object and the perceptible thing which, when it acts in an appropriate way upon our sense-organs, causes us to perceive it. There would appear to be only the following alternative answers to that question: either (i) the perceptible thing and the perceptual object are identical, i.e., they are one in every respect; or (ii) they are nonidentical, i.e., the perceptible thing and the perceptual object are two distinct entities, each having its own mode of existence. Adopting either horn of this dilemma leads to unsatisfactory consequences.

If the perceptible thing were in every respect identical with the perceptual object, then the perceptible physical thing would not exist when it is not perceived as an object. The perceptual object, we know, exists only as a result of the act of perception; hence when we are not perceiving, there is no perceptual object. If the perceptible thing were identical with the perceptual object, it would necessarily follow, then, that when we are not perceiving, there is no perceptible thing. We know this to be false with as much assurance as we know it to be true that when we are not perceiving there is no perceptual object. We are, therefore, compelled to conclude that the perceptible thing cannot be in every respect identical with the perceptual object.

The other alternative is equally unsatisfactory. If the perceptible thing and the perceptual object are two distinct entities, each having its own mode of existence (the one, real; the other, intentional), one of them could cease to exist while the other continues to exist. The perceptible thing that we think we are perceiving could cease to exist while, at the same time, the perceptual object continues in existence. The converse might also be the case: we could be actually perceiving the perceptible thing while, at the same time, the perceptual object might cease to exist. We cannot accept either of these diremptions between the perceptible thing and the perceptual object, diremptions which necessarily follow from the supposition that the perceptible thing and the perceptual object are two distinct entities, each having its own mode of existence.

As against the supposition that the perceptible thing and the perceptual object are completely identical, we know that perceptible physical things exist independently of their being perceived. They exist and are perceptible whether or not they are actually perceived. As against the supposition that the perceptible thing and the perceptual object are two entities, each having existence independent of the other, we know that the existence of the one (the perceptual object) depends on the existence of the other (the perceptible thing). Perceptual objects do not exist unless perceptible things are being actually perceived. We know, therefore, that the perceptible thing and the perceptual object cannot be completely identical, nor can they be completely distinct. What middle ground can there be between (i) complete identity and (ii) the nonidentity of two entities each of which can exist without the other? The solution of our problem would seem to lie in the answer to that question, if one is available.

Let me state the answer first and then try to explain it. Although the perceptible thing and the perceptual object are not completely identical they are sufficiently identical to be one entity having two modes of existence. If this were true, it would also be true to say that the perceptible thing can exist even when the perceptual object does not exist, but that the perceptual object cannot exist when the perceptible thing does not exist. We observe a certain asymmetry here in the relationship of perceptible thing and perceptual object, but it is precisely such asymmetry that accords with the facts as we know them, facts that are incompatible with both of the two suppositions that we found it necessary to reject.

To explain what has just been said, I must show that there can be a relationship that lies between complete identity and nonidentity—a degree of identity which, though incomplete, is nevertheless sufficient to preclude nonidentity. The explanation is as follows:

Two things, or, to be more precise, two aspects of one thing, are existentially inseparable in a symmetrical manner if neither can exist without the other, as is the case with the two faces of a coin. Though the two faces of a coin are aspects of it which are analytically distinct as heads and tails, they are existentially inseparable.

One and the same entity may have analytically distinguishable aspects (in this case, two modes of being) which are existentially inseparable, but only in an asymmetrical, not in a symmetrical, manner. In the case of the two faces of a coin, neither can exist without the other; hence their existential inseparability is symmetrical. The inseparability is asymmetrical rather than symmetrical, however, when what we are considering is one and the same entity with two modes of being—real existence as a perceptible physical thing and intentional existence as a perceptual object. On the one hand, since the entity can have real existence as a perceptible physical thing without being actually perceived, it can have real existence without also having intentional existence as a perceptual object. On the other hand, the entity cannot have intentional existence as a perceptual object unless it also has real existence as a perceptible physical thing. Its intentional existence is inseparable from its real existence, whereas its real existence is not inseparable from its intentional existence. This is just another way of saying that these two modes of being of one and the same entity are existentially inseparable in an asymmetrical manner.

Can we say anything more about the relationship of the perceptible thing and the perceptual object, to explain further what is involved in the partial yet sufficient identity of the two? In addition to their being one entity with two modes of existence which are inseparable in an asymmetrical manner, they also stand in a one-one relationship in a large number of respects, but not in all respects. Again we must recognize a partial, yet sufficient, identity of the two.

Consider a movable and perceptible thing and two observers of it, for whom it is one and the same perceptual object. A movement of the thing from here to there will be accompanied by a perceived movement of the perceptual object from one perceived place to another. If one of two observers were to pick up a stone and throw it over his left shoulder, and if he were then to ask his associate whether he observed

114

the flight of the stone, only to receive a reply in the negative, the person who threw the stone would know that the movable and perceptible thing was not one-one with a perceptual object which was common to his associate and himself. An affirmative answer, on the other hand, would indicate a one-one relationship between the perceptible thing and a perceptual object, which was the same object for two observers.

There can, of course, be unobservable or imperceptible changes in a physical thing, to which there will be no corresponding changes in the perceptual object. The converse would not seem to be true. Changes in the perceptual object will always correspond to changes in the perceptible thing or in the conditions of observation under which the perceptible thing is being observed. The one-one relationship is thus seen to be both asymmetrical and also partial. Nevertheless, there is a correspondence between the perceptible thing and the perceptual object in all those respects in which changes in the physical thing are perceptible; and this, together with the point previously made about the asymmetrical inseparability of the perceptible thing and the perceptual object, provides a basis for saying that they are sufficiently identical to be one entity having two modes of being—real existence, on the one hand, and intentional existence, on the other. In other words, one and the same entity is both a perceptible thing and an apprehended object, yet in such a way that its existence as a perceptible thing does not depend on its existence as an apprehended object.

The question about the precise character of the relationship between the perceptible thing and the perceptual object would now appear to be answered in a satisfactory manner—one that accords with all the facts as we know them. The answer, however, carries in its train certain difficulties which we must now try to overcome.

The first, and most important, difficulty concerns exceptions to a point of theory on which we have insisted as if it were without exceptions. I have said repeatedly that apprehending is not judging and does not involve affirmations or denials of the real existence of the object apprehended. (i) When a philosopher conceives God as that than which nothing greater can be conceived, he is merely apprehending God as an object of thought, and his apprehension is neither true nor false. The question remains open whether God, as an object thus conceived, really exists or not. If an affirmative answer to this question can be shown to be true, we then have knowledge that God exists; if it cannot be shown to be true, then we do not have knowledge that God exists. The mere conception of God as that than which nothing greater can be conceived does not give us such knowledge; nor is the conception affected by whether we can attain such knowledge or not. (ii) When a poet imagines the stately pleasure dome of Kubla Khan, he is apprehending an imaginary object which he probably knows is an entity that does not also really exist. Such knowledge of its nonexistence in no way affects the object of his imagination. His apprehension of it is neither true nor false, regardless of the truth or falsity of whatever opinion he might hold about the real existence of the entity which he is imagining. (iii) When a witness in court, under cross-examination, remembers this or that detail of an automobile accident, of which he happened to be an observer, his testimony concerning the speed with which one of the cars was moving expresses what is for him an object of memory. Another witness testifying at the same trial may express what is for him a different object of memory—a different speed of the car in question. When cross-examination tries to determine the credibility of the conflicting testimony, it is attempting to get at the factual truth about what really happened. Whether the jury decides in favor of one witness or the other, the remembered object for each of them remains the same, though what one witness claims to know in the light of his memory may be nearer to the truth than what the other witness claims to know in the light of his.

The three examples given above are perfectly representative of the sharp distinction between apprehending and judging in the spheres of conception, imagination, and memory. In each case, the entity conceived, imagined, or remembered is distinct from answers to questions about the real existence of the entity which is a conceptual, imagined, or a remembered object. The apprehended object is neither true nor false; truth or falsity belongs only to existential judgments—assertions of the real existence or nonexistence of the entity which is a conceived, imagined, or remembered object.

However, when we come to the fourth sphere of apprehension, that of perception, the relation between apprehending and judging seems to be radically different. When an observer says that he perceives a certain object, is he not also at the same time judging that his perceptual object is an entity that not only has intentional existence as an object but also real existence as a perceptible thing? Whereas it is relatively easy to separate conceiving, imagining, and remembering an object from making claims about the real existence of the entity that has intentional existence as an object of conception, memory, or imagination, it is relatively difficult, if not impossible, to make this separation in the sphere of perception. If we cannot make it, are we not obliged to concede that perception is a striking exception to an important tenet in our theory; namely, that apprehending is not judging and that apprehensions as such are neither true nor false?

To overcome this difficulty, by showing that what appears to be an exception is not really one, I must resort once more to the compatibility of analytical distinctness with existential inseparability. In the sphere of perception, (i) the act of apprehending an object and (ii) the act of judging that it is an entity which really exists are for the most part existentially inseparable while at the same time being analytically distinct. If the judgment that we always tend to make about the real existence of the entity that exists intentionally as an object of perception happens to be true, then we are at one and the same time engaged in the act of knowing the existence of a perceptible thing and in the act of apprehending a perceptual object. By maintaining the analytical distinction between these two acts, we can say that percepts, like concepts, images, and memories, are neither true nor false; nevertheless, we can also say that, unlike the acts of conceiving, imagining, and remembering, acts of perceiving are existentially inseparable from acts of judging, the products of which may be true judgments (knowledge) or false judgments (error).

The customary use of the word "perceive" confirms the point just made. When an individual says "I perceive X," he is, in effect, making two distinct statements, though he seldom keeps them distinct in his mind. He is saying (i) that he *apprehends* the object X, and (ii) that he *judges* that X is an entity which exists not only as an object but also as a thing. If the individual were not of the opinion that X is an entity which really exists, he would not use the word "perceive." As indicated above, the act of judging, which is existentially inseparable from the act of apprehending when that act is one of perceiving, does not necessarily produce judgments which are true. Such perceptual judgments may be false, in which case the individual's opinion that he is perceiving, and hence knowing, is in error.

Hallucinatory experiences provide us with cases in which the individual holds the erroneous opinion that he is perceiving when, in fact, he is not perceiving, but imagining. If the individual were of the opinion that he was imagining rather than perceiving, he would not be suffering from hallucinosis. His hallucinations consist in his apprehending an object concerning which he simultaneously forms the judgment that the entity apprehended also really exists. It may be difficult, if not impossible, to show him at the time that his judgment is erroneous and that he is imagining rather than perceiving; but normal persons in the room with the patient suffering hallucinations are certainly without doubt that the objects which he says he is perceiving are not perceptual objects, but objects of his imagination.

It may be asked what reason we have for thinking that we are not always hallucinating instead of perceiving. The answer, in part at least, turns on our ability to draw a fairly clear line between the normal and the abnormal. Hallucination, by definition, is an abnormal phenomenon—what might be called "aberrant perception," i.e., perception which only appears to be perception, but is not. Our opinion that we are perceiving rather than hallucinating gains strength simply from the number of other percipients who, with respect to a common perceptual object, hold the same opinion that we do, i.e., who, on perceiving that object, simultaneously judge that it is an entity which also really exists. Even one judgment to the contrary would challenge us to reexamine our opinion. A considerable number of adverse judgments would put us into a serious state of doubt.

The analytical distinction in the sphere of perception between apprehending and judging, accompanied by the existential inseparability of the act of apprehending from the act of judging, parallels the analytical distinction between the intentional and real existence of the entity which is both object and thing, accompanied by the inseparability of the objects's intentional existence from the thing's real existence.

V. Two Difficult Questions

Hallucination, as distinguished from veridical perception, provides us with the test case in which the judgment that accompanies the apprehension is false, and so the object regarded as perceptual is in fact not perceptual, but imaginary. In that case, the entity apprehended (by imagination) has intentional existence, but not real existence. It is the falsity of the judgment that makes the act of apprehension not an act of perception; but for the hallucinatory patient it remains an undetected counterfeit of perception until his judgment can be corrected and changed. He continues to think that he is perceiving a pink elephant over there in the corner of the room until he can somehow be shown that no pink elephant exists and none is over there.

Another example may provide us with an instructive illustration of the analytical distinction between apprehending and judging in the sphere of perception, combined with the existential inseparability of these two acts. A human being observed a half-mile in the distance is a perceived object of a certain very small size. The observer might be tempted to say "it looks like a speck," but his judgment would tell him that, if it were actually a speck, he could not see it at all a half-mile away. As the human being walks toward the observer and the distance closes, the perceptual object gets larger in size. The thing (in this case, a human being) is not getting larger in size, it is not changing, but the conditions (distances) under which it is being observed are changing, as the human being walks toward the observer; and corresponding to these changes in the conditions of observation (shorter and shorter distances) are changes of increasing size in the perceptual object. Throughout these changes, the observer is constantly judging that he is perceiving a man of normal size, not a speck that gradually gets larger and grows into a man. When the observed entity was at a great distance from the observer, he might have been in error in making the judgment that he was perceiving a man; but there could not even then have been any error about the size of the perceptual object that he was, correctly or incorrectly, judging to be a man far away. Throughout this series of changing perceptual objects, accompanied by an unchanging thing at changing distances, the perceptual object at each moment is always what it is, neither true nor false, but the judgment about it may be at one moment false (if the observer is of the opinion that the dis-

119

tant speck is not a man), and at another moment true (if the observer changes his opinion and judges that the larger perceptual object is an entity which is in fact a man).

Still another example having the same illustrative effect is provided by the familiar illusion of the straight stick which appears to be bent when it is observed immersed in a glass of water. Apprehended visually, the stick as a perceptual object is a bent stick; apprehended tactually, the same stick as a perceptual object is a straight stick. By taking the stick out of the glass of water, we know that our tactual perception is veridical and that our visual perception is illusory; we also know that the entity which really exists as a straight stick is, under certain conditions of observation (i.e., when immersed in water), a perceptual object that intentionally exists as a bent stick. By changing the conditions of observation, we can also change the character of the perceptual object without changing the character of the really existing thing.

We are able to construct diagrams which, in reality, have only one configuration, but which are so constructed that, without any change in the conditions of observation, we shift from one perceptual object to another—perceiving now a duck and now a rabbit. Neither is illusory, or both are; for the cleverly devised diagram either delineates both a duck and a rabbit equally well or it delineates neither.

One other difficulty remains. It parallels the one which has just been treated and, I hope, disposed of. In the exposition of the theory in the preceding chapters, the point was repeatedly made that naming is not asserting; and making this point rested on the distinction between apprehending and judging (or knowing, in those instances when the judgment is true). Just as an apprehension is neither true nor false, quite apart from whatever judgments may be made about the object apprehended, so the words or phrases which name apprehended objects are neither true nor false, quite apart from whatever sentences may be constructed which make assertions that are either true or false.

The statement just made certainly holds for words or descriptive phrases that name conceptual objects or objects of memory and imagination. But does it hold for words or descriptive phrases that name perceptual objects, i.e., does it hold for the proper name or definite description that applies to a unique particular, designating it not merely as one of a kind, but as a unique one of that kind? Can we use a proper name or definite description without at the same time asserting that the singular perceptual object so named is an entity that also really exists?

The solution of this problem is, in principle, the same as the solution already advanced. Just as, in the sphere of perception, the solution consists in seeing that apprehending and judging, while existentially inseparable, are analytically distinct, so here, in the sphere of language, the solution consists in seeing that naming and asserting, while existentially inseparable in our use of proper names and definite descriptions, are nevertheless analytically distinct. It is possible to concoct pseudo-proper names, or deceptive definite descriptions, just as it is possible to suffer hallucinations and, in consequence, be led to false judgments about what really exists.

A pseudo-proper name or deceptive definite description might mislead someone into thinking that the particular object named or described was an entity that really existed, but the error would be an error in the assertion accompanying the use of the name or description, not an error in the name or description itself. A writer might invent a fictional character and give that fictional character a proper name, but so construct his narrative as to give the impression that the story being told is historical, not fictional, with the result that a reader might be misled into thinking that a pseudo-proper name denoted a really existing individual. That existential denotation, however, would have to be expressed in a proposition which asserted the existence of the subject term, expressed verbally by a proper name, pseudo or genuine. If pseudo, the existential proposition would be false; if genuine, true. But in either case it is the sentence, not the name, which expresses the assertion and is either true or false.

The analysis just given holds for deceptive definite descriptions, e.g., "the present king of France." That phrase names a conceivable particular and, in addition, a unique one. If, however, that unique particular cannot be a perceptual object, because no present king of France really exists, then propositions are false which, in the course of characterizing the present king of France as bald, fat, or stupid, also assert his existence in reality. The conjunction—(i) There is a present king of France *and* (ii) he (the present king of France) is bald—is false

121

because the first member of the conjunction is false. If the second member can be separated from the first, as well it might be by a person who, imagining a present king of France, imagines him as bald, then the second member of the conjunction is not false. By itself, it makes no existential assertion, particularly if the person uttering the judgment guards himself by adding "I am not saying whether there is or is not a present king of France; I am only talking about an object of my imagination." In the light of the foregoing, it should be clear that what we know to be a deceptive definite description is not itself false, for it has existential denotation only when it plays the role of the subject in an affirmative existential proposition; and it is only the latter which is false when its subject term is a deceptive definite description.

Six.
Discourse
about Objects of Perception,
Memory, and Imagination

Preamble

The preparation laid down in the preceding chapters will enable me to answer with brevity the questions to be raised in this chapter and in the chapter to follow.

In this chapter we will be concerned with special questions about the use of language to talk about matters that fall within the sphere of perception, memory, and imagination; and in the next chapter we will deal with conversation about matters that fall within the sphere of conceptual thought. In the one case, we are concerned with discourse about particulars; in the other, with discourse about universals.

Since, as I pointed out earlier, the particular is never an unclassified or uncharacterized individual but always one of a kind, or of a number of kinds; universals are always implicitly present in the particular objects of perception, memory, and imagination; conceptual thought is always operative in acts of perceiving, remembering, and imagining.

On the other hand, universal objects can be apprehended quite apart from the apprehension of the actual or possible particulars that do or can instantiate them; and, in addition, there may be universal objects which are incapable of instantiation.

The questions which concern us here are as follows: 1. In our conversations about objects of perception are we also talking to one another about really existent things? 2. Can one and the same object of discourse be a perceptual object for one person, a remembered object for another, and an imagined object for a third? 3. Can we discourse about imaginary objects that are never objects of perception or memory?

Question 1. In our conversations about objects of perception are we also talking to one another about really existent things?

In my answer to Question 2 in Chapter V, I began by saying that it is only in the case of perception that we have the pervasive and almost incorrigible impression that what we are perceiving is a really existent thing and not an object having intentional existence. As the answer to Question 2 developed, two things became clear: first, that, while the physical thing and the perceived object are analytically distinct, the perceptual object is existentially inseparable from the physical thing; and, second, that in the sphere of perception, the acts of apprehending and judging, while analytically distinct, are also existentially inseparable.

With regard to the first point, it should be recalled that the existential inseparability of the physical thing and the perceptual object is less than complete identity: the two are not one-one in all respects; the inseparability is asymmetrical, the perceptual object depending for its existence on the existence of the physical thing, but not the other way around. The analytical distinction is a distinction in aspects of one and the same entity which as physical thing has one mode of being (real existence) and as perceptual object has another (intentional existence).

With regard to the second point, it need only be remembered that, whereas naming is not asserting, the naming of a perceptual object cannot be separated from an assertion that the object named is an entity which also has real existence. The abnormal phenomena of hallucination confirm this. The patient with *delirium tremens* judges that what he imagines really exists and, therefore, he regards himself as perceiving and not as imagining. In other words, to regard one's self as perceiving, even when one is not, is to attribute real existence to the entity that is the object being apprehended. The object being apprehended remains exactly the same whether the accompanying judgment is true, as in the normal case, or false as in the case of the person suffering hallucinosis.

The person who is hallucinating may certainly be said to have the illusion that he is perceiving rather than imagining. That, however, would appear not to apply to the rest of us. Yet there is still one respect in which the rest of us suffer an illusion, which is pervasive and almost incorrigible. It does not consist in our regarding the object of perception as an entity which really exists, but rather in our obliterating the distinction between that entity's intentional existence as a perceptual object and its real existence as a physical thing. When we regard ourselves as perceiving we are so overwhelmingly persuaded of the real existence of the entity being perceived that we suppose ourselves to be in direct contact with an unobjectified reality. The illusion we suffer is that, when we perceive the book we are holding in our hand, our perception, no less than our hand, puts us into direct contact with the thing-as-such. The illusion is cured by reinstating the perceptual object as the mode of existence which the entity being perceived possesses when, and only when, it is being perceived; it is then not the thing-as-such but the thing-as-apprehended; but it always remains the case that the thing-as-apprehended also really exists as a thing-as-such, for its real existence in no way depends upon its being apprehended.

It follows, therefore, that in our conversations about objects of perception, we are talking to one another about entities which are not only perceptual objects, but are also really existent things. To say that we are talking only about entities which are perceptual objects would be as much in error as to say that we are talking only about entities which are really existent things. We are talking about both at once because they are inseparable aspects of one and the same entity. Yet, while inseparable, they are analytically distinct. This, for the most part, we tend to forget, which is just another way of saying that, for the most part, we persist in allowing the perceptual illusion to go uncorrected. Nevertheless, there are the striking exceptional cases which remind us that the perceptual object is not perfectly identical with the physical thing.

Consider the case of two men talking about a straight-edged ruler which they have immersed in a glass of water. One handed the ruler to the other. The ruler, passed from one to the other, is one and the same physical thing physically handled by both of them. It is common to both of them in the sphere of action. The ruler having been immersed in a glass of water by the man to whom it was passed, the two now talk about its appearance. They agree that the ruler appears to be bent when observed under the optical conditions created by immersion; they also agree that the ruler taken out of the glass of water, or perceived by touch rather than by sight, appears to be straight; and, finally, they agree that the latter appearance accords with the way in which the ruler really exists as a physical thing because (i) they know that it was manufactured to be a straight-edged instrument of measurement and (ii) they know about the optical distortion produced by certain conditions of observation.

The two men engaged in such conversation cannot help but acknowledge that the ruler—one and the same entity for both of them—has two modes of being which are analytically distinct: on the one hand, its being as a really existent physical thing; on the other hand, its being as an intentionally existent perceptual object when it is visually observed in a glass of water. If one of the two men engaged in conversation had been congenitally blind, the bent ruler as a perceptual object for the man with sight could not have been a perceptual object for the blind man. The latter, however, listening to a verbal description given him, might have been able to imagine a bent ruler in tactual terms. As their conversation proceeded, they would certainly have acknowledged that one and the same entity, the ruler, is a physical thing common to both of them and also a perceptual object for each of them, the same perceptual object for both by tactual apprehension, but not the same perceptual object by the one's tactual apprehension and by the other's visual apprehension. In any case, it will be clear to the two men that they must make an analytical distinction between the ruler as a really existent thing and the ruler as a perceptual object, the ruler being one and the same entity under two aspects.

When, in discourse, we use proper names or definite descriptions which we have imposed on unique particulars in the sphere of perceptual objects, these words or phrases not only refer to the perceived object, but they also simultaneously denote the existent thing. Just as, in the sphere of perception, the acts of apprehending and judging, or of naming and asserting, are inseparable while remaining analytically distinct, so, for the same reason, the referential significance of proper names or definite descriptions is inseparable from their existential denotation.

Yet they are always analytically distinct, as we can discover in the case of mistakes in the use of what only *appear* to be proper names or definite descriptions. When we discover such mistakes, the referential significance of the pseudo-proper name or the crypto-definite description remains unaltered: it still signifies or refers to an apprehended object. The discovery of the mistake leaves the referential significance unaltered, but removes the existential denotation of the word or phrase. The word or phrase in question still names the same object, but the existential assertion which accompanied the naming is now known to be false, not true.

A proper name or definite description always signifies or refers to a unique particular, not just to any one of a kind, but to this one alone. That unique particular may be an object of perception, but it need not be. Unique particulars can be objects of memory or of imagination as well as of perception. The question of whether a proper name or definite description is genuine or deceptive (i.e., whether it has existential denotation as well as referential significance; whether it names an entity that not only exists intentionally as an apprehended object but also has had or can have real existence) is a question to be faced in the sphere of memory and imagination as well as in the sphere of perception.

There is more to be said on this point in the answers to Questions 2 and 3. Here I wish only to call attention to the special significance of the demonstrative pronouns "this" and "that." When they occur in definite descriptions, such as "this chair on which I am now sitting" or "that table over there at which I am now pointing," the definite descriptions thus constructed always refer to perceptual objects, never objects of memory or imagination. This is tantamount to saying that the use of "this" or "that," accompanied by a physical action on the part of the user, such as sitting or pointing, always combines existential denotation with referential significance. The perceptual object referred to is always also an entity that really exists here and now; the naming of the object by a descriptive phrase is inseparable from attribution of real existence to the entity which is a perceptual object.

Question 2. Can one and the same object of discourse be a perceptual object for one person, a remembered object for another, and an imagined object for a third?

To answer this question, it is necessary to make it more explicit on two points. The first point is that the ideas which are products of the acts of perceiving, remembering, and imagining must be as distinct in character as the acts themselves are. A percept is not a memory, an image is not a percept, and so on. Hence the question being asked can be rephrased in the following manner: Can ideas as distinct in character as a percept, a memory, and an image present to the minds of three persons one and the same object, so that the words they use in discourse with one another all refer to an object that is common to the three of them?

The second point assumes an affirmative answer to the question just asked, and asks further whether the object that is an object of perception for one person, an object of memory for another, and an object of imagination for a third, is an entity which also really exists. It obviously cannot be a genuine perceptual object unless it does; but we know that an object of memory or an object of imagination can be an entity which does not really exist. However, unless the object that is a common object of discourse for three persons, each of whom apprehends it in a different manner, is also an entity that really exists, the conversation we are considering could not take place, since one of the three persons is apprehending that object perceptually.

One example will suffice to support an affirmative answer to the question that has now been fully elaborated. Let the physical thing in question be the wallpaper on a woman's bedroom. The woman is sitting in her bedroom looking at the wallpaper while talking about it on the telephone to her husband. For her the wallpaper is a perceptual object; for him, it is a remembered object. Though the woman and her husband are operating with ideas which are not only numerically distinct but are also distinct in character (one a percept, the other a memory), the two ideas can be the same in intention and so can present the same object to their minds. Furthermore, if it is one and the same object that both are apprehending, though by different modes of apprehension, then it must also follow that the object being remembered by the husband must be an entity that also really exists, since that same object is an object being perceived by his wife. If that object were not an entity which also really existed, she could not be perceiving it. So far, then, we are able to say that the wallpaper has two modes of existence: real existence on the wall and intentional existence as both a perceptual and a remembered object.

A little later the wife telephones a friend of hers and discusses the wallpaper, asking for advice about putting wallpaper of the identical pattern on the guest-room wall. The friend says that she has never seen the wallpaper in question. The wife then tells her friend that the pattern is the same as that of wallpaper on the friend's bedroom wall, except that the pattern is red on white, not blue on white. At this point the friend says that she can imagine the wallpaper and recommends putting it on the guest room wall.

For the friend, the wallpaper is neither a perceived nor a remembered object. It is an imagined object. Though an image is different from a percept and a memory, it can nevertheless be the same in intention, and so be able to present the same object to the mind of the friend that is present to the wife through perception and to the husband through memory. It is thus one and the same object of discourse for all three of them. In addition, because it is an object of perception for one of them, that which is a common object for all three of them, though differently apprehended, must be an entity which also has physical existence on the bedroom wall. This is tantamount to saying that it is quite possible not only to remember but also to imagine an object that is an entity which also really exists.

If two persons are talking about an object which is an object of memory for both of them, an object of imagination for both, or an object of memory for one and an object of imagination for the other, the question about whether that common object is an entity which also really exists, which also once existed, or which also may exist in the future, cannot be so easily answered.

Let us consider first the case of two persons, both of whom are remembering the same object. That object may be an entity which now really exists and is, therefore, capable of being perceived by a third person. If that third person is not a party to the conversation, the conversation of the two persons about what at first appears to be a common object of memory requires them to exercise two cautions. First, they must make a discursive effort to be sure that their numerically distinct memories are the same in intention, with the result that the object each is remembering is present to them as a common object about which they can talk. They can do this by asking each other questions about the object being remembered and thus become satisfied, with reasonable assurance, that it is the same object for both of them. Second, they must not be precipitate in judging whether the remembered object is an entity which either now really exists or once really existed and no longer does. Assuring themselves that they are both remembering the same object is hardly assurance that the object remembered is an entity that either has or had real existence. They could both be utterly deceived on this score, or be in some degree of error.

If they are not deceived or in error, and if the object which they are commonly remembering is an entity which once had real existence but no longer really exists, can we say that one and the same entity has both intentional existence as an apprehended object and real existence as a thing? The answer must be negative since we know that the object being remembered is an entity which no longer really exists. Nevertheless, it once did really exist. The fact that its two modes of existence are *not simultaneous*, as they are in the case of perception, does not alter the underlying principle. In the case of perception, the perceptual object is an entity which has both intentional and real existence at the same time, i.e., it really exists at the same time that it is being perceived; whereas in the case of memory, the object remembered may be an entity which had real existence at an earlier time but now no longer has it, and now has only intentional existence for those who remember it.

What has just been said applies to the case of two persons, both of whom are imagining the same object. They must exercise the same cautions in order to be sure that the object each is imagining is common to them both; and in order to discuss the question whether that common object is an entity which may also have real existence at some future time. Such a discussion, for example, might take place about an invention which they are commonly imagining. If they concur in the judgment that the particular piece of apparatus which they have used their imaginations to invent is an imagined object which is also capable of real existence in the future, the principle already stated applies; namely, that an entity which now has only intentional existence as an object of imagination may at some future time also have real existence as a physical thing.

The case of a conversation between two persons about an object that one of them is remembering and the other imagining raises no new considerations. The same cautions must be exercised; the same principle applies.

Question 3. Can we discourse about imaginary objects that are never objects of perception or memory?

The power of the imagination is not limited to making objects of entities that have existed, do exist, or can exist in reality. It can construct and produce objects that no one can remember or perceive because they are entities which have never existed, do not now exist, and cannot exist. Let us call such objects "imaginary objects" in contradistinction to imagined objects, including among the latter not only an object like the wallpaper which one person perceives, another remembers, and a third imagines, but also the imagined apparatus which, when produced by its inventor, will have real existence in the future.

Imaginary objects, which can also be called "fictions of the imagination," are entities which have only one mode of existence—intentional existence. That in itself does not prevent them from being common objects of discourse. What is an imaginary object for one person can be an imaginary object for another, if one person's power of verbal description is capable of instigating in another person the constructive acts of imagination required for producing it. The only person for whom an imaginary object is an object of acquaintance rather than an object of description is the person who is its author—the person by whose imagination the imaginary object was originally constructed. Anyone else will have to depend upon the author's verbal description of the imaginary object in order to produce it for himself; and when it is so produced it will be an object of description rather than of acquaintance.

Let us consider first an example which I have touched on in another connection—the case of the patient suffering *delirium tremens* and having the hallucination that there is a pink elephant or a purple tiger in a menacing posture in the corner of his room. The attendant psychiatrist listens to the patient's description of the imaginary object produced involuntarily by hallucinosis. Depending on the vividness and the detail of that description, the psychiatrist may be able to conjure up either the same imaginary object or a fairly close approximation to it, sufficient for the purpose of a conversation between the patient and the psychiatrist about the pink elephant or the purple tiger. That conversation, of course, cannot go beyond reference to this or that characteristic or changing feature of the imaginary object they are discussing. While the hallucination is in progress, the psychiatrist will not be able to convince the patient that the pink elephant or purple tiger is only an imaginary object and not a perceptual one.

Of all the creative arts, literature alone, because language is its medium, produces imaginary objects or fictions of the imagination which can be communicated descriptively. The poet, novelist, or dramatist describes a fictional character which is the product of his imagination (Captain Ahab, for example, in *Moby Dick*, or for that matter, the white whale itself); or he describes some imaginary entity or place (the stately pleasure dome of Kubla Khan in Xanadu) which his imagination has produced. Depending on their powers of imagination, and the assiduity of their efforts, the readers of his work will be able to produce for themselves the same imaginary objects, or at least to achieve close approximations to them, sufficient for the purposes of conversation.

Such conversations take place, in manifold forms and myriad instances, whenever human beings talk to one another about books they have read. The fact that Captain Ahab or that the singular white whale does not really exist, and never will exist, does not prevent persons from talking about these objects as common objects of reference, just as they talk about the incumbent President of the United States, or about Abraham Lincoln, or the white horse that George Washington rode, or the crossing of the Delaware at Valley Forge. If it were thought to be impossible for persons to converse about the imaginary objects initially produced by poets and writers of fiction, one would be forced to the contrafactual conclusion that a teacher of literature and his students could never engage in a discussion of a work that all of them have read. One need only think of the countless hours which have been devoted by students, teachers, literary critics, and others to the discussion of the character and actions of Shakespeare's Hamlet, to dismiss as preposterous even the faintest suggestion that imaginary objects cannot be common objects of discourse.

The mention of Shakespeare's Hamlet raises for us one final question about objects in the realm of the imaginary. Some of them, like the fictions of mythology (e.g., Cerberus or Charon), bear proper names that do not appear in the pages of history; but some, like Hamlet and Julius Caesar, appear in Shakespeare's plays and also in writings that are usually not regarded as fictional. The proper name "Hamlet" can be used to refer not only to the character created by Shakespeare, but also to refer to what may be regarded as his prototype in the *Historiae Danicae* of Saxo Grammaticus, a twelfth-century Danish historian; in addition, if the account of Saxo Grammaticus is reliable, "Hamlet" was the proper name of a singular prince of Denmark, who lived at a certain time and was involved in regicide, usurpation, incest, rape, and all the rest of it. So, too, "Julius Caesar," as a proper name, refers to at least three different singular objects: (i) the leading character in a play by Shakespeare, (ii) an historical figure described in one of Plutarch's *Lives,* and (iii) the Roman general who lived at a certain time, who conquered Gaul, wrote a history of his battles in that province, crossed the Rubicon, and so on.

Do proper names, such as "Hamlet" and "Julius Caesar," used in the triplicate manner indicated above, refer to one singular object or to three? The fact that the same word is being used as a proper name in all three cases does not give us the answer. The same words, functioning as proper names, are frequently repeated in a telephone book, and we know that they denote different actual persons from the fact that, attached to each of the seventy-five John Smiths we find, there are different addresses and telephone numbers. Just as we use an address that we know to be his, in order to select the one John Smith we wish to telephone from all the others, so we must use definite descriptions to identify the singular object we wish to talk about when the proper name of that object is also capable of being used for other, quite distinct, singular objects.

If we wish to talk about the character and actions of Julius Caesar as portrayed in the play of that title by Shakespeare, we must identify the imaginary object of our discourse by a definite description of it as "the character of that name in a play by Shakespeare, with the title, 'Julius Caesar,' first produced on such a date, etc." It would be confusing, indeed, if one of two persons who are engaged in a conversation about Julius Caesar used that proper name to refer to Shakespeare's Julius Caesar and the other used it to refer to Plutarch's Julius Caesar. They might get to the point of making contradictory statements about the apparently common object of their discourse, only to find that they did not have a common object, but were in fact talking about different objects—objects which resembled one another in certain respects, but which differed in others.

That Shakespeare's Julius Caesar is an imaginary object of discourse, no one will question. The fact that there are certain resemblances between Shakespeare's Julius Caesar and Plutarch's and also between Plutarch's Julius Caesar and Rome's Julius Caesar, who was general, first consul, and temporary dictator in the years

59 B.C.–47 B.C., does not change the status of Shakespeare's invention. His Julius Caesar is a fiction of the imagination no less than Cerberus and Charon. Are we, by the force of this argument, led to the same conclusion about Plutarch's Julius Caesar and, therefore, about all of the historical personages described by historians and biographers?

The same difference exists between Rome's Julius Caesar and Plutarch's Julius Caesar as exists between Rome's Julius Caesar and Shakespeare's Julius Caesar. If we believe that a singular man, named Julius Caesar, actually lived in Rome at a certain time, performed certain actions and occupied certain offices, then we also believe that Rome's Julius Caesar was once an object of perception. Other men were directly acquainted with him, and the object with which they were directly acquainted was also an entity which had real existence. But Plutarch's Julius Caesar, like Shakespeare's, can only be apprehended by description, never by acquaintance. To that extent they are alike as imaginary objects—fictions of the imagination. However, they are also unlike Captain Ahab in Melville's *Moby Dick,* or Raskolnikov in Dostoevsky's *Crime and Punishment.* The latter, as fictions of the imagination, have no prototypes in historical personages, whereas both Shakespeare's Julius Caesar and Plutarch's Julius Caesar do.

In making this last point, I am passing from the consideration of the character of objects as apprehended to the state of our knowledge about the objects in question. Viewed strictly as objects apprehended, Greek mythology's Cerberus and Charon, Plutarch's Julius Caesar and Shakespeare's, Melville's Captain Ahab and Dostoevsky's Raskolnikov, are all imaginary objects—fictions of the imagination. None, precisely as described, ever was or can be an object of perception. But we do affirm, as a matter of historical knowledge, that there was a singular historical personage, bearing the proper name "Julius Caesar," who was an object of perception at a certain time in the city of Rome. In contrast, we do not affirm, as a matter of historical knowledge, that there ever were such personages as Captain Ahab or Raskolnikov. Therein lies the difference between one type of imaginary object and another. It is not a difference in the object as apprehended, but rather in the judgments we make about them: for example, that Shakespeare's Julius Caesar resembles, in certain definite respects,

Plutarch's Julius Caesar; and that these points of resemblance include characteristics which the best historical evidence available has established as matters of fact.

One other difference between the poet and the historian should be noted. Shakespeare invented a dramatic character to which he gave the name "Julius Caesar" and whom he portrayed in a certain definite way. Understanding his craft as poetry rather than history, Shakespeare nowhere made any existential assertions about his Julius Caesar, nor did he offer any evidence to support the truth of statements made about him. In his play, the proper name "Julius Caesar" has referential meaning only, no existential denotation: it functions solely to signify a fiction of the poet's imagination. But Plutarch, in his life of Julius Caesar, does offer evidence of the truth of statements of historical fact about the man whose biography he is writing; and so, either explicitly or in effect, Plutarch makes existential assertions about Julius Caesar. Therefore, in Plutarch's biography, the proper name "Julius Caesar" has both referential meaning and existential denotation—referential meaning as signifying an imaginary object constructed by Plutarch but not purely a fiction of his imagination; and existential denotation when it is used as the subject in propositions having existential import, which Plutarch asserts.

There has been little difficulty in showing that imaginary objects can be common objects of discourse. However, in the course of establishing that point, we have discovered certain difficulties to be overcome in discourse about such objects, particularly in those cases in which the same word or set of words is used as a proper name for a number of different imaginary objects, and for both an imaginary object and an object which once was an object of perception.

Seven.
Discourse
about Objects of Thought

Preamble

The answer to Question 1 in Chapter IV enumerated posits required for the solution of the problem of meaning. Among these was the distinction between acts of perception, memory, and imagination, on the one hand, and acts of conception, understanding, or thought, on the other. The objects apprehended by acts of the first sort are all particulars; the objects apprehended by acts of the second sort are universals—kinds or classes in which particulars participate as members, or of which they are instances.

The general solution of the problem of meaning involves the voluntary imposition of meaningless notations upon objects apprehended by acts of the mind, with the result that the meaningless notations acquire referential significance and so become name-words that signify or refer to the objects upon which they have been imposed. If objects which are the referents of name-words were all of the same sort, it would be impossible to explain the difference between the referential significance of proper names and definite descriptions, on the one hand, and common or general names and indefinite descriptions, on the other.

The most cursory consideration of ordinary discourse will reveal that men use proper names or definite descriptions to refer to singular particulars, not just one of a kind, but a unique one; in contrast, common names or indefinite descriptions are used to refer to kinds or classes—universals. Hence the reason given for positing the distinction between (i) the objects of perception, memory, and imagination and (ii) the objects of conception, understanding, or thought was its indispensability for explaining the difference in the referential significance of (i) proper names and (ii) common names. The posited distinction was strictly a posteriori, i.e., made solely for the purpose of explaining what calls for explanation, not made on grounds independent of any consideration of the phenomena of language and human discourse.

This posited distinction, however, is denied by philosophers who come to their consideration of language with a definite commitment to an opposite view of the human mind—one which sees it as more homogeneous in character, all its ideas or apprehended objects being particulars of one sort or another: particulars perceived, particulars remembered, particulars imagined. The philosophers who make this prior commitment then undertake to examine language and human discourse and try to explain the meaning of common or general names without appealing to universal ideas or objects as the referents of such words. If they could succeed in this effort, then our position on the matter would be refuted; for it would have been shown that it is not necessary to posit a distinction between acts of the mind which apprehend particular objects and acts of the mind which apprehend universal objects in order to explain the difference between the referential significance of proper and common names.

At the opposite extreme, other philosophers have held the view that reality itself is divided into two realms—the realm of sensible or perceptible particulars, on the one hand, and the realm of intelligible universals, on the other. It is difficult to determine whether those who hold this view do so entirely apart from the consideration of language and human discourse. In any case, this view, whether from the point of view of a philosophy of language it is a posteriori or a priori, would appear to provide an alternative explanation of the difference in referential significance between proper and common names. It must, therefore, be considered in relation to the position we take on this matter.

These alternative views will be considered in the answers to Questions 1 and 2. A third alternative which might be mentioned need not be considered, for it involves a proposed solution of the problem of meaning which has already been shown to be untenable; namely, that meaningless notations acquire their referential significance by being imposed by the individual on his own subjective ideas (see Chapter III, Question 3). Since philosophers who take that view of the matter cannot account for the communicative use of language, we need not consider their theory of the referential significance of common or general names, which is that they refer to general or, as they are sometimes called, abstract ideas. This is not to deny that there is a difference between (i) ideas produced by acts of perception, memory, and imagination and (ii) ideas produced by acts of conception, understanding, or thought, a difference that is commensurate with the difference between their objects—(i) particular objects, on the one hand, and (ii) universal objects, on the other. There must be such a difference; but it is not the difference between percepts and concepts that explains the difference between proper and common names, but rather the difference between perceptual and conceptual objects.

With the rejection of alternative solutions accomplished in Questions 1 and 2, I will then turn to other problems concerning objects of thought as objects of dicourse. I will deal with these problems in the following order: 1. Can the meaning of a common name be explained in any other way than by a universal object of thought as its referent? 2. Are universal objects of thought entities that also have real existence? 3. Can all universal objects of thought be instantiated by perceived or perceivable particulars? 4. How can two or more persons assure themselves that the conceptual object signified by a common name they are using is one and the same object for all of them?

Question 1. Can the meaning of a common name be explained in any other way than by a universal object of thought as its referent?

I have already made sufficiently clear that the meaning of a proper name (or its equivalent, a definite description) lies in its reference not just to a particular, any one of a number or variety of particulars, but to this one and this one alone, which we should speak of as a *singular* particular to emphasize its *uniqueness*. That is the referential significance of each person's own proper name, of the proper names of his relatives and friends, and of such proper names as "Julius Caesar" and "Hamlet," or of such definite descriptions as "the incumbent President of the United States in 1943" or "the chair on which I am now sitting."

As I will subsequently point out, in the answers to Questions 3 and 4, common names divide in a number of ways: (i) some, such as "man," "dog," "tree," or "chair," signify kinds or classes which can be directly instantiated by perceptual objects; (ii) some, such as "justice," "freedom," "meson," and "infinity," signify universal objects which cannot be instantiated in that way; and (iii) some, such as "centaur" and "mermaid," signify kinds or classes that cannot be instantiated at all. The objects signified or referred to by these different types of common names are all equally objects of discourse—objects about which men talk to one another, agreeing and disagreeing about them in a wide variety of ways.

For our present purposes, it will be best to confine our attention to common names of the first type, for it is with respect to them that the argument concerning alternative explanations of their referential significance can be carried on most clearly. In ordinary discourse, a common name, such as "man," "dog," or "chair," is used in two ways: (i) it is used in the presence of a particular man, dog, or chair as a perceptual object; and (ii) it is used when no particular instance is being perceptually apprehended. When we say "I see a man coming down the lane," we are using the common name "man" in the first way; when we say "men differ in intelligence as well as in height," we are using the plural form of the word "man" in the second way.

The same distinction holds for indefinite descriptions. In the statement "I see a dog that looks like a poodle coming down the lane," the indefinite description "a dog that looks like a poodle" is being used in the first way to signify a perceived particular of a certain kind. In the statement "poodles are a non-hair-shedding breed of dog," the indefinite description "a non-hair-shedding breed of dog" is being used in the second way to signify a kind of dog, but without reference to any perceived particular.

How do those philosophers who deny that the human mind apprehends universal objects by its acts of conceptual thought explain the referential significance of common names or indefinite descriptions, considering for the moment only common names of the first type and only as used in the first way to designate perceived particulars? The philosophers in question admit the distinction between proper and common names, sometimes calling the latter "general names" to indicate that they apply to more than a single particular. They admit that words like "dog" or "poodle" apply to a number of perceived particulars; but they deny that the world includes among its constituents any entities that can be characterized as universals rather than as singular individuals; and they also deny that, among the mind's ideas or its objects, there are any that can be characterized as general or universal rather than as particular. If the contrast between a general and a particular idea is stated in terms of the difference between abstract and nonabstract ideas, these philosophers deny the existence of abstract ideas; if it is stated in terms of a sharp difference between concepts, on the one hand, and percepts or images, on the other, they deny that such a difference exists. How, then, do they explain the referential significance of such words as "dog," when it is used in the statement "I see a dog coming down the lane"?

The explanation such philosophers offer is as follows. They say that a common name, such as "dog," is a general name, or a name that is general in its reference, because we apply it to any one of a number of particulars indifferently, i.e., without discriminating between this particular and that one in any way that would make the word "dog" inapplicable to both of them. The general significance of the word "dog" is such, they hold, that I can use it today when I see a poodle coming down the lane and tomorrow when I see an airedale coming down the lane, on both occasions being equally able to say "I see a dog coming down the lane." If, on both occasions, another person is present who hears my statement but is not looking in the same direction, he will understand that I am referring to a particular dog, but he will not know without looking whether I am referring to the same dog as yesterday or a different dog. Either is possible.

The explanation offered, upon examination, reduces to the statement that a common or general name is one that can be applied to two or more individuals which are the same (not different) in a certain respect, or which have some characteristic or characteristics in common. To affirm this statement is, of course, tantamount to acknowledging that the two or more perceptual instances to which a common name can be applied are improperly called "individuals." They are particulars, each a unique or singular particular, but each a particular, nevertheless, in that it has something in common with the other particulars to which the common or general name applies. If all these particulars did not have something in common, or were not the same in certain respects, then one and the same common or general name could not be correctly applied to all of them *indifferently,* as the philosophers who take this view insist.

If, at this point, the philosophers in question were to deny that two or more entities (whether called by them "individuals" or "singulars") can be the same in any respect, or have anything in common, then the only explanation they have to offer would be undercut, and they would leave us with no explanation at all. Let us suppose, therefore, that the philosophers in question do not go to the extreme of denying that two entities can have anything in common or be the same in any respect. We are, therefore, obliged to ask them whether we are able to apprehend what is common to two or more entities, or apprehend the respects in which they are the same. If their answer to this question is negative, they have again completely undercut their own explanation of the meaning of common names as applicable to two or more items *indifferently* (i.e., in respect to some point in which they are *not different);* for if we cannot apprehend any respect in which two or more items are the same, we cannot apply one and the same name to them indifferently. The only alternative left open to them is an affirmative answer to the question: Are we able to apprehend what is common to two or more entities, or apprehend respects in which they are the same?

If the philosophers in question give that affirmative answer, because they must either give it or admit that they have no explanation to offer, then the giving of that answer is tantamount to a refutation of their original position. To affirm that what is common to two or more entities, or that what is the same about them, can be apprehended, is to posit an object of apprehension which is quite distinct from the object apprehended when we perceive this or that singular particular as such. But this is precisely the position which we maintain is the correct solution of the problem; namely, that there are objects of apprehension other than perceived particulars. Yet it is precisely this which the philosophers in question initially denied by asserting that there is nothing general in the world except words.

I have considered the one use of common names which is easiest to explain—the use in which they are applied to perceived particulars which are indifferently instances of a certain kind or class of entities. If the philosophers in question cannot explain that use of common names without refuting themselves, a fortiori they will be even more hard-pressed when confronted with the problem of explaining the use of common names to signify kinds or classes quite apart from perceived particulars, and still more so when the reference is to kinds or classes that do not or cannot have perceptual instances.

Before I leave the consideration of a position that I regard as untenable in a philosophy of language which attempts to explain the meaning of words, I wish to comment briefly on the strange persistence of a philosophical view that is plainly self-refuting. I have in an earlier chapter called attention to the persistent error in modern thought of regarding either ideas or their objects as representations of reality—of things as they really exist in total independence of the human mind (see Chapter IV, Questions 3 and 4). In view of the disastrous consequences to which this error has led, its persistence is difficult to understand. But it is even more difficult to understand the persistence of the erroneous view that there is nothing general in the world except words. That view, which had its origin in the Middle Ages, has flourished in modern times and is still a widely prevalent view in spite of the fact that any extended statement of it turns out, upon examination, to be self-refuting.

One additional remark is relevant here. The view that has been rejected as untenable does not originate in a philosophy of language which takes the explanation of meaning as its primary problem. It originates in the context of ontological and psychological doctrines which are elaborated quite apart from any consideration of language. The consideration of language is then undertaken in the light of these prior ontological and psychological commitments, with results which can only be described as procrustean. We submit that if these prior ontological and psychological commitments had been avoided, and if the question about universal ideas (i.e., concepts) or about the universal objects apprehended by such ideas were initially raised in the context of a philosophy of language, the result would be the view that is here adopted; namely, that universal objects, conceptually apprehended, must be posited in order to explain the referential significance of common names, and for no other reason.

The last point just made has a direct bearing on the other alternative view that we should consider, the view, namely, that intelligible universal entities (sometimes called self-subsistent "ideas" or "forms") exist in reality, as a distinct domain from that of perceived particulars, which are also entities that exist in reality. Either (i) this view is developed in the context of a philosophy of language and, therefore, as an a posteriori posit required to explain the meaning of common names; or (ii) it is developed as an ontological doctrine quite apart from considerations about language and the meaning of words. Regarded in either way, it is highly questionable, though not self-refuting.

Regarded in the first way, it is questionable because it violates the principle of parsimony: *it posits more than is needed* for the solution of the problem of the meaning of common names. The positing of universal objects of thought as the referents of such words suffices for that purpose. The additional posit of really existent universal entities, therefore, cannot be justified; and so is highly questionable.

Regarded in the second way, as an ontological doctrine independent of the consideration of language and meaning, the view is questionable because of its psychological consequences. If really existent perceptible entities are the cause of acts of perception, whereby we apprehend these same entities as perceptual objects, should it not be the case that really existent intelligible entities cause acts of understanding or thought whereby we apprehend those same entities as conceptual objects? Why, on the contrary, do our acts of conceptual thought appear to depend upon our experience of perceptual objects, the memory of them, or even the imagination of them. Why, further, in the case of the simplest common names, such as "man," "dog," or "tree," do they appear to acquire their referential significance initially by being applied to a number of perceived particulars, understood to be all of one kind, instead of being applied directly to the universal kind which really exists in and of itself?

When I say that the philosophical doctrine under consideration is highly questionable, I am saying no more than that the foregoing questions are extremely difficult to answer, if in fact they are answerable at all. In addition, I surmise that this questionable philosophical doctrine would never have originated in the first place were it not for the general or universal significance of common names, especially such words as "justice," "truth," "being," and "good." If that is in fact the case historically, then our first argument against the theory of self-subsistent ideas or forms is reinforced. The theory asserts the existence of a realm of entities that need not be posited to explain the meaning of such words, or of any other common names which signify common objects of human discourse.

If we reject one alternative theory as untenable because it is self-refuting, another (the one which posits an individual's own abstract ideas as the referents of the common names he uses) as incapable of explaining the communicative use of language, and the remaining third alternative, just considered, as either unjustified or highly questionable, we are left with the only solution of the problem which can be regarded as tenable in itself and also as capable of explaining how men use common names to talk to one another about objects of thought. That solution consists in asserting that universal objects apprehended by conceptual thought are the referents of common names.

Question 2. *Are universal objects of thought entities that also have real existence?*

Having rejected the view that reality includes a realm of self-subsistent universal entities as well as a realm of individual things, let us ask: Is there any other way in which the universal objects of thought to which our common names refer can have a foundation in reality? Are conceptual universals, unlike perceptual particulars, entities that exist only intentionally as objects of apprehension?

Perceptual particulars, we have come to understand, are entities that exist simultaneously both as things and as apprehended objects; i.e., both really and intentionally. Many of the objects we remember are entities that no longer really exist, but once existed. We imagine objects which are entities that do not exist and sometimes cannot exist. In all these cases, the intentional existence of the object apprehended in one way or another suffices to account for the referential significance of name-words and for the communicative use of language. Why, then, is it not sufficient to affirm the intentional existence of the universal objects apprehended by conceptual thought? What is the reason for a further concern about their relation to reality, i.e., their relation to things in the realm of real existences?

That further concern centers on acts of knowing involving universal objects. The existential propositions which we affirm or deny do not exclusively consist of statements in which the subject terms are expressed by proper names or definite descriptions referring to perceptual particulars. They include a wide variety of statements about kinds or classes of entities which, either implicitly or explicitly, involve assertions or denials of the real existence of particular instances of the kind or particular members of the class being referred to.

Logicians distinguish between propositions having existential import, such as "some swans are white," and propositions which do not have existential import, such as "angels are messengers of God," or "all men are mortal." In the first case, what is being asserted is twofold: (i) particular swans exist, and (ii) some of them are white. In the second case, what is being asserted is that to be an angel is to be a messenger of God, or that to be a man is to be mortal, the truth of which does not depend on there being any angels or any men. We can conceive kinds which are in fact null classes (i.e., classes without really existent members), and we can make statements about the properties or characteristics of the kind of entity that we have conceived. We can also make statements of this sort when we are in doubt about whether the kind conceived is a class which has or can have really existent members; and the truth or falsity of these statements will be independent of further questions about the real existence of particular instances.

What has just been said suggests the answer to the question which concerns us here. In the case of particular objects of memory and imagination, we can ask whether the objects apprehended are entities that do exist in reality, have existed, or can exist; but we cannot ask that precise question in the case of the universal objects of thought. We can ask only whether particular instances of these objects exist in reality, may exist, or can exist. In other words, we can ask only whether the kind or class of entities that we have conceived is in fact instantiated, or can be instantiated, by particulars which are apprehended by perception or in some other way and which, in addition, are entities that really exist.

A further problem must be considered. Let us take, for example, the universal object to which the common name "swan" refers. That word names a kind which has instances in reality, a class which has really existent members. To say that each of these instances is a particular swan is also to say that each participates in whatever is common to all swans, whatever is the same about all of them. Were there nothing common to all swans, or the same about them, this entity and that could not be apprehended as particular swans. To apprehend an entity as a particular of a certain kind involves an apprehension of the kind itself, and that in turn depends on the apprehension of what is common to or the same about a number of items or entities. When, in the case of the kind named by "swan," particular instances really exist, must it not also be true that the sameness which unites the really existent instances as particular swans is a sameness that really exists in them?

Philosophers have given opposite answers to this question. Some affirm the reality of what is common to or the same about the members of a class, or instances of a kind. In doing so, they affirm a foundation in reality for the universal which is a conceptual object, without going so far as to affirm that the universal really exists in and of itself. What is being affirmed is only that the universal really exists *in* particular instances as that which is common to them or the same about them. What is one and the same in two individuals may necessarily be a diversified or individuated sameness; nevertheless, its presence is sufficient to establish the fact that the two individuals share something in common.

The opposite answer, which denies that what is common to or the same about particular instances of a certain kind really exists *in* them, confines the universal to the realm of objects having intentional existence, without any counterpart in the realm of really existent things.

The issue joined by these conflicting answers is, perhaps, one of the most difficult problems for philosophers to resolve, but a resolution of it is not required for the philosophy of language. To account for the significance of common names, and for their use in referring to public or common objects of discourse, it is (i) necessary only to acknowledge the intentional existence of universal objects apprehended by conceptual thought. To account for the distinction we make between statements which have and statements which do not have existential import, and to understand questions about the relation of conceptual universals to perceptual particulars, it is (ii) necessary only to recognize that some conceptual universals are actually instantiated, some may or may not be instantiated, some can be instantiated, and some are incapable of being instantiated by entities which really exist and are or can be apprehended by perception. To go beyond these two points is not necessary for an adequate philosophy of language.

It may not always be the case that a conceptual object is instantiated by perceived particulars which really exist. It may sometimes be instantiated by remembered particulars which once existed, or by imagined particulars which may exist in the future, or even by imagined particulars that cannot really exist at all. For example, we can imagine particular mermaids or particular centaurs in order to instantiate the conceptual object signified by the word "mermaid" or "centaur." We will return, in answering Question 5, to the consideration of these and other conceptual objects which do not and cannot have instantiation in reality. For the moment, suffice it to say that of all the objects that can be produced by acts of conceptual thought, only some are conceptual universals that are or can be directly instantiated by perceptual particulars which have real as well as intentional existence. Typical examples of this group are the objects of discourse referred to by such common names as "man," "dog," "tree," "chair," "green," "heavy," "square," "running," "standing," "sitting," and so on.

To sum up: universal objects are always the referents of common names, but sometimes the common name, having such a referent, is applied to apprehended particulars (whether perceived, remembered, or imagined), as instances of the kind or class conceived. When a common name is applied to particular instances, it must be emphasized that the referent is not the particular as a unique singular, but rather the particular as an instance; or, in other words, the universal as instantiated. In all other cases, common names refer to universal objects without regard to the particulars that do or may instantiate them.

It should be added that when a common name occupies the position of the subject term in an affirmative existential proposition which is true, it has existential denotation as well as reference to an apprehended universal object. What it denotes is the set of actually existing entities which are particular instances of the kind or class signified by the common name.

Question 3. Can all universal objects of thought be instantiated by perceived or perceivable particulars?

Grammarians have distinguished between what they call "concrete" and "abstract" common names. They use the word "concrete" to designate that class of common names, such as "man," "dog," "tree," "chair," which can be applied to perceived particulars as instances of a certain kind; and, in contrast, they use "abstract" to designate that class of common names which cannot be so applied; for example, "freedom," "justice," "infinity," "n-sided polygon," and so on.

This traditional distinction can be translated into the difference between those universal objects of thought which are capable of being instantiated by perceptual particulars and those which cannot be. We cannot perceive particular instances of infinity, freedom, justice, or an *n*-sided polygon; nor can we imagine or remember them. Are we to conclude that common names of the latter sort cannot be instantiated at all? The answer is affirmative in the case of common names which signify mathematical objects, such as "infinity" or "*n*-sided polygon," but that answer is subject to certain qualifications when we consider such common names as "freedom" and "justice."

In discussing freedom or justice, it is certainly possible to give examples of the universal object that is before our minds by describing a man in a particular setting as being free or unfree, or by describing a man performing a certain act as being just or unjust. These examples will usually be products of imagination or of memory, but it is not impossible for them to be perceived situations or actions. Nevertheless, it would be incorrect to say that we are perceiving, remembering, or imagining particular instances of freedom or justice, as if they were like particular instances of such universal objects as dog, tree, or chair. What should be said here is that the universal object can be exemplified in a particular case which we are able to perceive, remember, or imagine.

Mermaids and centaurs are imaginary objects, or fictions of the imagination (see Chapter VI, Question 3). They are entities which have intentional existence only, no existence in reality. Yet particular centaurs or particular mermaids have been depicted in illustrations of mythology or imaginative literature. This should not lead us to the conclusion, however, that when we look at such pictures, we are perceiving particular instances of the universal object mermaid or centaur. These universal objects are conceptual fictions, just as the particular mermaid or centaur that we may see in a picture or read about in mythology is a fiction of the imagination. To speak of them as conceptual fictions is to say that they are universal objects which are not only incapable of being instantiated by perceptual particulars, but also incapable of being exemplified in particular cases which we are able to perceive, remember, or imagine.

The universal objects of mathematics and logic form still another group of conceptual objects that cannot be instantiated by perceptual particulars. We are often misled into thinking that the diagrams we see in a treatise on geometry are perceived instances of the mathematical objects being discussed; it would be more correct to treat them as imagined helpful examples rather than as perceived instances. In any case, there is a large number of mathematical objects which cannot be exemplified in any way, for the object being conceived is not only an entity that is imperceptible but also one that is unimaginable.

In an earlier tradition, such universal objects were called *"entia rationis"* or "beings of reason" to signify that the entities in question had intentional existence only and no existence in reality; that is, no instantiation in reality. The group of objects traditionally called *"entia rationis"* included conceptual fictions, negations or privations, and second intentions; and among second intentions were the objects of mathematics and logic. Some versions of the traditional theory of second intentions have held that second intentions constituted an exception to the rule that concepts are never objects that we apprehend. The objects of mathematics and of logic, this view maintained, were concepts that we apprehend and refer to by the technical terms of those sciences.

With regard to this view, two points must be made. First, there are no exceptions to the principle that concepts or percepts are intrinsically inapprehensible. They are not in any way objects which we can inspect or examine. While each of us is reflexively aware of the acts of his own mind, no one is reflexively aware of the ideas produced by mental acts; it is only the objects of ideas that we apprehend or are aware of. Second, it is true that the universal objects of mathematics and logic differ from the universal objects of other sciences, usually called "empirical" because they deal with observable phenomena as perceived instances of the universal objects to which their basic technical terms refer. It is this difference which must be explained without conceding that concepts are ever objects that we apprehend. The explanation is as follows:

To grasp the distinction between first and second intentions, let us consider these two statements: (i) "Men are animals," and (ii) " 'Man' is the predicate in the proposition 'Socrates is a man'." In the first of these two statements, the common names, "men" and "animals," are both being used in the first intention. In the second statement, the common name "man" is being used in the second intention reflexively and the common name "predicate" is being used in the second intention attributively. When a common name is used in the first intention, the universal object to which it refers is being considered as having or as being capable of having instances in reality, or at least as being capable of exemplification in particular cases. But when a common name is used in the second intention reflexively, the universal object it refers to is being considered in and of itself, and without regard to instantiation or exemplification.

All the technical terms used in mathematics—common names that refer to the conceptual objects of that science—are words being used in the second intention reflexively. Mathematical discourse is not about the concepts of mathematics, as an erroneous view of second intentions would have us suppose; it is about the conceptual objects of mathematics considered in and of themselves, and without regard to instantiation or exemplification. In addition to being the objects of second intentional reference, the universal objects of mathematics are also *entia rationis;* for, strictly speaking, even so simple a mathematical object as the right triangle has no perceived instances in reality, even though the mathematical truths which we know about the right triangle are, in some measure of approximation, applicable to physical triangles.

Any common name in the vocabulary of ordinary discourse or in the technical terminology of a science can be used in the second intention reflexively as well as in the first intention. But for the most part, common names are used by ordinary speakers and by scientists, with the exception of mathematicians and logicians, almost exclusively in the first intention. We have already seen that the technical terms of mathematics are common names which are used in the second intention reflexively. It is primarily the logician, concerned with the conceptual objects of other sciences, who uses ordinary as well as technical common names in the second intention reflexively; and it is only the logician who has a technical vocabulary of his own which consists of common names that must be used in the second intention attributively and can be used in no other way.

The example we have already employed should suffice to make this clear. We said that in the statement " 'Man' is the predicate in the proposition 'Socrates is a man'," the term "predicate" is being used in the second intention attributively, for it places the term "man" in a certain logical category. Such common names as "subject" and "predicate" are logical terms: they categorize the logical status or role of the terms to which they are applied, and these other terms, thus categorized, must be common names used in the second intention reflexively, for it is the conceptual object in and of itself which is being categorized logically.

Failure to observe whether terms are being used in the first or the second intention can result in fallacious reasoning. From the statement "Socrates is a man" conjoined with the statement " 'Man' is a predicate," we cannot validly infer that Socrates is a predicate. The first of the two statements, which might be made in ordinary discourse, is a statement in the first intention; whereas the second statement, which is strictly a statement in logic, is in the second intention.

Parallel to the distinction between first and second intentions is another distinction in the use of words—that between first and second impositions. We use a word in the first imposition when we use it to refer to an apprehended object of one sort or another. We use a word in the second imposition reflexively when we use the word to refer to itself; and we use a word in the second imposition attributively when we use it to categorize or characterize another word as an object of discussion. For example, when we say "Man is an animal," we are using the words "man" and "animal" in the first imposition: we are using them to refer to the universal objects which they signify, objects which can be instantiated by perceptual particulars. In contrast, when we say that "man" is a three-letter word, or an English word, or a noun, we are using the word "man" in the second imposition reflexively in order to talk about that word itself as an object of discourse. Words such as "noun," "verb," or "particle," are common names which can be used only in the second imposition attributively; that is, they can be used only to categorize or characterize other words as objects of discourse.

Just as fallacious reasoning results from failure to observe the distinction between statements in the first and statements in the second intention, so, too, fallacious reasoning results from failure to observe the distinction between statements in the first and statements in the second imposition. From the statement "This apple is red" conjoined with the statement " 'Red' is an adjective," we cannot validly infer that this apple is an adjective.

Recognition of the use of words or phrases in the second imposition reflexively enables us to solve a problem which so sorely puzzled an eminent modern logician and philosopher of mathematics that he chose to reject the doctrine that common names refer to universal objects rather than accept what he thought to be an inevitable tenet of that doctrine. He was puzzled by the significance of the phrase "round square." Does it refer to a universal object of thought, in the same way that "right triangle" or "*n*-sided polygon" does? If so, then the realm of universal objects includes entities that are self-contradictory in addition to entities that have no instantiation in reality, such as conceptual fictions. Rather than accept a conclusion so repugnant to reason, the thinker in question preferred to reject the whole doctrine of the intentional existence of universal objects as referents of the common names employed in ordinary discourse, in the empirical sciences, and even in such sciences as mathematics and logic.

The solution of the problem raised by a phrase such as "round square" involves no puzzlements, paradoxes, or conclusions repugnant to reason. We can talk about that phrase by using it in the second imposition reflexively; and, using it thus, there is only one thing to be said about the phrase "round square," namely, that, beyond referring to itself when it is used in the second imposition reflexively, it signifies nothing that is perceptible, imaginable, or conceivable. Even if the question whether a square can be constructed which has an area equivalent to the area of a given circle were to be answered affirmatively (which, of course, it cannot be), it would still remain the case that the phrase "round square" has no referential significance at all, for there is no perceptible, imaginable, or conceivable object that it can refer to. It is a meaningless grammatical construction: its two components, "round" and "square," are meaningful words, not nonsense syllables; but when they are conjoined in a phrase which is supposed to function like a common name or indefinite description, that phrase has no referential significance.

If an entity is that which has some mode of existence, either real or intentional, or both, then a round square is a non-entity. It has no mode of existence, not even intentional, for it cannot be an object of thought. What has just been said applies without qualification to all phrases which are grammatically constructed by the conjunction of meaningful words which separately refer to objects of thought that cannot be conjoined because each excludes the other. Speaking on the plane of second impositions, we can say that phrases which are constructed out of words that refer to objects which must be related disjunctively rather than conjunctively cannot have any referential significance.

Question 4. How can two or more persons assure themselves that the conceptual object signified by a common name they are using is one and the same object for all of them?

In the sphere of perceptual objects, what has been called "ostensive definition" enables two or more persons to identify the common object to which they are severally referring. The entity which is the perceptual object referred to by such definite descriptions as "my automobile," "the chair I am now sitting on," or "that book over there on the table" can be pointed to or otherwise indicated in some nonverbal manner. The persons engaged in talking about the object in question can thus nonverbally identify the really existent entity that is inseparable from the object to which their words refer.

Such ostensive identification—it is more precise to call it identification rather than definition—establishes the public or common character of the object. Resort to ostensive identification in the sphere of perceptual objects enables those engaged in conversation to test and certify that the words or phrases they are using to name such objects signify common objects of reference. When I can point to or otherwise indicate in some nonverbal manner the really existent entity that is also the perceptual object which your words and my words refer to, I am assured not only that it is an entity which is common to us in the realm of action, but also that it is an entity which is common to us in the realms of cognition and discourse.

Ostensive identification is not available to us in the sphere of remembered and imagined objects, except for the case in which the object remembered or imagined by one person is identical with the object perceived by another (see Chapter VI, Question 2). Nor is ostensive identification available to us with regard to all those objects of thought which are not capable of perceptual instantiation. What devices, then, can we resort to in order to assure ourselves of the public character of a large number of objects of discourse—objects of memory, imagination, or thought which are not capable of perceptual instantiation? How can you and I be sure that we are talking about one and the same object when we use words to refer to objects that we can remember or imagine but cannot perceive; or to objects of thought that do not have perceptual instances?

The importance of this problem cannot be overestimated, especially in its application to universal objects of conceptual thought. We have rejected the theory that the words a person uses refer to his own ideas on the ground that reference to subjective ideas makes the communicative use of language impossible. This would remain the case even if subjective ideas could be apprehended and words could refer to them, which they cannot (see Chapter III, Question 3). The reference of words to apprehended objects accounts for the communicative use of language, but only if the objects referred to are common or public—intersubjective, not subjective as a person's own ideas are. Hence we must face the problem of how, in the absence of ostensive identification, we can assure ourselves that when you and I use common names we are referring to conceptual objects that are common to both of us.

The first step in the solution of this problem is a relatively easy one. A certain number of common names, those which have been called "concrete," refer to universal objects which are capable of being instantiated by perceptual particulars. For such common names (e.g., "man," "dog," "tree," "chair"), something like ostensive identification of the object being referred to is possible. To be sure that you and I have the same universal object in mind when we use a word like "dog" or "chair," I can point to a particular dog or a particular chair, or to several particular dogs or chairs, all objects of perception; and I can accompany that nonverbal indication of a perceptual instance or perceptual instances by the question, "Is the entity pointed to a perceptual instance of the conceptual object you are referring to when you use the word 'dog' or the word 'chair'?" An affirmative answer from you should give us both sufficient assurance that the conceptual object referred to is one common to us both.

Further conversation may reveal that your understanding of the object referred to does not coincide with mine in all details; but given the initial assurance that it is the same object for both of us, we can at least try to overcome, by further conversation, the differences that may exist in our judgments about it. I may come to agree with your detailed characterization of the object; you may come to agree with mine; or we may continue to differ, but that difference can constitute a genuine disagreement only on the basis of its being a difference concerning one and the same object of discourse.

The part of the problem which remains unsolved concerns those common names that refer to objects of thought which may be capable of instantiation, but for which no perceptual instances are now available; and, beyond that, common names which refer to objects of thought which cannot be instantiated at all because they are kinds which cannot have perceptual instances. The solution will be found, I suggest, in the method of nonostensive identification set forth in the two-volume study of *The Idea of Freedom*, published by the Institute for Philosophical Research.

Before I summarize that method, it may be instructive to point out that when the word "idea" is used in such phrases as "the history of ideas" or "the great ideas," or in the titles of books, such as "The Idea of Freedom," "The Idea of Justice," or "The Idea of Progress," it does not signify the subjective ideas which are the immediate products of the mind's acts, but rather the objects apprehended by means of those subjective ideas. To make this quite clear, let me translate all the phrases and titles mentioned above into phrases and titles which more accurately state what is involved. In place of the title "The Idea of Freedom," I propose "Freedom as an Object of Thought." Not only is this more accurate, but, in addition, it stresses the use of the word "freedom" in the second intention. A book on freedom as an object of thought treats that conceptual object *in and of itself;* similarly in the case of justice, progress, or love as objects of thought, treated in books which are entitled "The Idea of Justice," "The Idea of Progress," or "The Idea of Love." In place of the phrase "the history of ideas" or the phrase "the great ideas," I propose, as more accurate even if somewhat more laborious to say, "the history of the objects of conceptual thought," or "the great objects of conceptual thought."

The group of scholars at the Institute who were engaged in research on freedom as an object of conceptual thought explored a vast literature on that subject, a literature which clearly contained references not to one object of thought, but to several distinct objects, all named by the single word "freedom," or its synonym "liberty." The researchers found it possible and necessary to identify five distinct conceptual objects which the word "freedom" or "liberty" has been used to signify in the tradition of Western thought. The identification was established by discovering the distinctive notes which constituted the connotation of each of the five objects, and then by verifying the identifying connotation by recourse to the literature being studied. Each of the five freedoms which has been an object of conceptual thought was identified by notes that belong to it alone and are not shared by any of the other four objects. As contrasted with the method of ostensive identification which can be employed in the case of perceptual particulars, the method which must be employed in the case of universal objects of conceptual thought can be described as a method of connotative identification.

Attention should be called to two additional points. First, when an abstract common name, such as "freedom," is used to signify a number of distinct conceptual objects, it is necessary to avoid misleading equivocation in the use of the word, as well as to show that the five uses of the word are not completely equivocal because a thin thread of common notes runs through the connotations of the word in all five uses.

To avoid misleading equivocation, qualifiers must be added to the word "freedom," such as "circumstantial freedom of self-realization," "acquired freedom of self-perfection," "natural freedom of self-determination," "political freedom," and "collective freedom." These five phrases, functioning as common names or definite descriptions, refer to five distinct objects of thought, each of which has been an object referred to by certain authors and not by others who have written on the subject of human freedom. Only by thus identifying and naming the five distinct objects is it possible to discover which authors join issue with one another in genuine disagreement about the object of their thought. If one group of authors is discussing the circumstantial freedom of self-determination and another group is discussing the natural freedom of self-determination, they cannot be in genuine disagreement with one another, even though they may appear to be because they are all using the single word "freedom" and saying opposite things about the object to which they are referring when they use that word.

To show that the use of the word "freedom" to signify five distinct objects of thought does not involve the kind of complete equivocation that occurs, for example, when the word "pen" is used at one time to signify a writing instrument and at another time to signify an enclosure for pigs, it is necessary to discover and formulate the connotative identification of freedom as a generic conceptual object under which the five distinct conceptual objects fall as modes or types of freedom. If this can be done, then the literature on the subject has a coherence that it would lack if there were no common notes underlying the five freedoms which have been connotatively identified as distinct objects of thought.

The second point to be observed is that the distinction just made between the ostensive identification of perceptual particulars as common objects of reference and the connotative identification of conceptual objects as common objects of discourse parallels the distinction made earlier between naming by acquaintance and naming by description (see Chapter III, Question 5). The objects that we name by acquaintance are either the particular objects that we can apprehend by perception or the universal objects that we can instantiate by perceptual particulars; and such objects are always objects that we can ostensively identify as common objects of reference and of discourse. In contrast, the objects that we name by description are either objects of memory and imagination which cannot be apprehended by perception, or objects of conceptual thought which cannot be instantiated by perceptual particulars; and these, in turn, are objects that we must identify connotatively in order to assure ourselves that they are common objects of reference and of discourse.

The same point can be stated in still one other way. Common names fall into two groups: (i) those which initially acquired their referential significance by being imposed on perceived instances of the kind signified, instances which are objects of acquaintance; and (ii) those which initially acquired their referential significance by a verbal description of the universal object—the kind or class—on which the name was imposed. Common names in the first group refer to universal objects which can be ostensively identified, just as the singular objects referred to by proper names or definite descriptions can be ostensively identified. Common names in the second group refer to objects of thought which must be verbally described by the method of connotative identification.

The method of connotative identification may be laborious and may require sustained critical discourse for its successful employment. Nevertheless, the method is, in principle, used in ordinary discourse and not just by scholars engaged in philosophical research or in the study of a body of literature dealing with objects of conceptual thought. It is resorted to in our daily conversations with one another. You ask me what I have before my mind when I use a certain common name. In response to that question, I try to do what I can to identify verbally the universal object I am referring to. I may not always succeed, but I do succeed frequently enough to show that universal objects of thought can be connotatively identified to become common objects of reference.

When we succeed in this process of connotative identification, you and I have sufficient assurance that a common name we are using refers to an object that is the same object for both of us, so that we can genuinely disagree with one another about its characterization in detail. With such success, common names, having reference to universal objects of thought, serve the purposes of communication. When we fail in this process, as happens often enough, our failures should not be attributed to insurmountable obstacles, but rather to our lack of skill, or our lack of patience and persistence, in making the effort required to accomplish the verbal identification of a universal object of thought.

Epilogue

*T*he modern failure to develop a
sound philosophy of language is the story of little errors in the beginning which have had disastrous consequences in the end. Most of these
little errors have been pointed out in the preceding chapters of this
book, and most of them have been corrected by the posits required for
a solution of the basic problem in the philosophy of language, a solution which accounts for the use of language as an instrument of communication, both in ordinary and in philosophical discourse. The
philosophical consideration of language has been one of the dis-
tinguishing features of modern thought; but, beset by errors which are
also characteristic of modern thought, it has failed signally.

Of all the little errors in the beginning that have plagued modern
philosophy from the outset, the most serious one is the one that was
made in the theory of cognition. It was first made by Descartes, but the

most compact expression of it is to be found in the Introduction to John Locke's *Essay Concerning Human Understanding.* Though the error originated with Descartes, not with Locke, it was the influence of Locke's psychology on Berkeley and Hume, and through Hume on Kant, that led to all the many times multiplied errors which spring from one little error in the beginning.

In the last paragraph of his Introduction, Locke writes:

> Before I proceed on to what I have thought on this subject, I must here . . . beg pardon of my reader for the frequent use of the word *idea,* which he will find in the following treatise. It being the term which, I think, serves best to stand for whatsoever is the *object* of the understanding when a man thinks, I have used it to express whatever is meant by *phantasm, notion, species,* or *whatever it is which the mind can be employed about in thinking.* . . . I presume it will be easily granted me that there are such *ideas* in men's minds; every one is conscious of them in himself; and men's words and actions will satisfy him that they are in others. Our first inquiry then shall be, how they come into the mind.

A careful reading of this paragraph will disclose a number of points. (1) It is evident that Locke went to school at Oxford with tutors who were scholastics, for it must have been thus that he acquired such terms as "phantasms" and "species" and learned that they stood for factors in the cognitive process. Either he was a poor student or his scholastic instructors were poor representatives of that tradition, for it is also clear from the passages quoted that he did not learn the most important things the tradition could have taught him about the cognitive process.

(2) It is evident that Locke uses the word "idea" to stand for something private: the ideas in one man's mind are not identical with the ideas in another man's mind. Each man has his own. Each of us, according to Locke, is conscious of his own ideas, and can directly apprehend only his own ideas. Each of us must infer from the speech and actions of others that other men have ideas in their minds, too.

(3) What each of us directly apprehends—the objects of our apprehension, says Locke—are always and only our own ideas. But

Locke also implies that these ideas come into our minds from without. As Book II of the *Essay* makes amply clear, the ideas in our minds, the objects we directly apprehend, are caused by things outside our mind—real existences of one sort or another which we cannot directly apprehend. In fact, as many passages reveal, Locke believed in the real existence of Newton's world of bodies in motion, ultimately composed of imperceptible atomic particles. It is the action of these on our corporeal organs that somehow produces the ideas that are the objects of our minds whenever we are engaged in thinking.

(4) As the passage quoted indicates, and as the rest of the *Essay* fully substantiates, Locke makes no distinction between the sensitive and the intellectual powers. He merges them into one cognitive faculty which he calls "understanding" or "mind." Though he uses the term "abstract ideas" instead of "concept," an abstract idea for Locke is a product of the same faculty that produces what others would call "sensations" and "perceptions" or "phantasms." If he had used the word "concept" instead of "species" in the paragraph quoted, we would read him as saying that both phantasms (or percepts) and concepts are *ideas,* without any differentiation between them.

The points made in (3) and (4) above reveal the presence of two little errors, not one. The first is the error of regarding ideas as the objects that we directly apprehend when we are conscious—thinking or dreaming. The second is the error of failing to distinguish sense and intellect, or perceptual and conceptual thought. While they are cooperative in the cognitive process, they do not operate in the same way, nor do they contribute in the same way to whatever knowledge we are able to achieve. These two errors together led to the nominalism of Berkeley and Hume; to the idealism of Berkeley and to the phenomenalism of Hume; to Kant's efforts to extricate philosophy from these consequences by trying to circumvent them with an ingeniously confected theory of mind, instead of by correcting the little errors from which they arose. They led to all the riddles and perplexities of later empiricism concerning the subjective and the objective, concerning our knowledge of the external world, concerning the logical construction of "objects" which we cannot directly apprehend from the sense-data which we do directly apprehend, concerning the referential meaning of words which do not have directly apprehended sense-data as their referents, and so on.

To avoid the solipsism which is inherent in Locke's premises, along with the extreme skepticism which Hume saw was a conclusion from these premises but which he tried to avoid, it was necessary to regard ideas—the only objects we directly apprehend—as somehow *representations* (copies, counterparts, or resemblances) of real existences which we cannot directly apprehend. Neither Locke nor Hume, each self-imprisoned within the world of his own ideas, had any hesitation in talking about a world of things which are not ideas—an independent world of nature or reality which would exist and be whatever it is regardless of the existence of the human mind and its cognitive acts. How regarding private ideas in our own minds, as directly apprehended objects and also as representations of things which cannot be directly apprehended, enables us to have knowledge of or even a rational belief in an independent world of real existences is a mystery that has remained unsolved. The futile attempts to solve it have produced a variety of other mysteries, resulting in obscurities and perplexities that have riddled philosophy in the nineteenth and twentieth centuries.

Kant, instead of correcting the errors made by Descartes and Locke, and instead of rejecting the problems raised by Hume in consequence of those errors, tried to circumvent Hume's conclusions by philosophical inventions specifically designed for that purpose. Post-Kantian thought, both in the nineteenth and twentieth centuries, was not only a record of diverse reactions to Kant's inventions, but also a record of self-defeating attempts to solve problems that would not have been problems at all if the errors initially made by Descartes, Locke, and Hume had been corrected.

From that false start, modern philosophy has never recovered. Like a man who, foundering in quicksand, compounds his difficulties by struggling to extricate himself, Kant and his successors have multiplied the difficulties and perplexities of modern philosophy by the very strenuousness—and even ingenuity—of their efforts to extricate themselves from the muddle left in their path by Descartes, Locke, and

Hume. The only way out of the debacle of modern philosophy is to go back to its beginning and try to make a fresh start, not in the way that Descartes proposed, by razing all prior philosophical constructions to the ground, but rather by going back to prior insights which, if heeded, might have saved modern philosophy from getting off the track.

The fresh start which should be made lies in an insight that would have prevented the error committed by Descartes and Locke. We can find it compactly expressed in a single paragraph of the *Summa Theologica*, a paragraph which stands in striking contrast to the paragraph quoted earlier from Locke's *Essay*. In Part I, Question 85, Article 2, Aquinas rejected the errors of those who, in the objections raised, said that sensible and intelligible species (i.e., in our terms, percepts and concepts) are that which we perceive and understand. On the contrary, he wrote, "the intelligible species is to the intellect what the sensible species is to sense. The sensible species [i.e., the percept] is not what is perceived, but rather that by which we perceive. Similarly, the intelligible species [i.e., the concept] is not what is understood, but that by which we understand."

The simple distinction between that which is apprehended and that by which it is apprehended corrects the error of Descartes and Locke. It should be noted at once that we are here referring only to the first act of the mind, the act of simple apprehension, and to its products—its percepts, memories, images, and concepts; we are not referring to the subsequent acts of the mind, its acts of judgment and of reasoning. The act of simple apprehension, in which sense and intellect cooperate while remaining distinct, is not an act of judging. It is only when we claim to know, by judging and reasoning, that we either do know and make true judgments, or fail to know and make erroneous ones. Simple apprehension involves no judgments and so is neither true nor false.

It is not enough to see that the distinction, in the sphere of simple apprehension, between that which we apprehend and that by which we apprehend it, removes the error made by Descartes and Locke in regarding ideas as the objects apprehended and also as representations of the real existences about which we seek to make true judgments and thus come to know. It is also necessary to understand what is involved in rigorously adhering to the view that ideas (percepts, memories, images, and concepts) are always and only that by which we apprehend, never that which we apprehend.

The first thing which must be understood is that the products of our mind's first acts—its percepts, memories, images, and concepts—are totally unexperienceable, uninspectable, inapprehensible. We can never experience, inspect, or examine them; for they are always and only that by which we apprehend whatever it is that we do apprehend, and never that which we do apprehend. The second thing which must be understood is that, by means of our ideas as instruments of apprehension, we apprehend a variety of objects—perceived objects, remembered objects, imagined or imaginary objects, and conceived objects or objects of thought. The third thing which must be understood is that these apprehended objects are not representations of things, or real existences of any sort. The objects of our apprehension are entities which always have intentional existence; they may, in addition, be entities which also have real existence, but that is not always the case.

All of these points have been fully elaborated in the preceding chapters and do not need further discussion here. They are mentioned here only to summarize what is involved in making a fresh start by rigorously adhering to the distinction between that which is apprehended (objects) and that by which they are apprehended (ideas); the distinction between the intentional existence of objects and the real existence of things; the distinction between apprehension and judgment; and the distinction between perceptual and conceptual thought. All of these distinctions were lost or obscured in the tradition of modern philosophy which began with Descartes and Locke. It is only because it has recovered them and put them to work that the present book can claim to have produced the rudiments of a sound and adequate philosophy of language.

In addition to being beset by errors in the theory of cognition, the modern consideration of language began with two philosophers whose innovations did not bear fruit until the present century. One was Hobbes; the other, Leibniz. Not until the twentieth century did the philosophical approach to language take its direction from the proposals of Hobbes and Leibniz. Then these two proposals were combined to constitute an approach to language that has provided the controlling framework within which virtually all philosophical discussions of language have taken place in the English-speaking world during the last seventy years.

In my judgment, the innovations made by Hobbes and Leibniz constitute a false start in the philosophy of language itself—another set of little errors which should have been corrected instead of having their consequences fully developed. It is the development of their consequences in the present century which has produced what, in my judgment, is an unsound and inadequate philosophy of language.

Hobbes proposed the view that words have meaning only when they refer to physical existences, i.e., bodies perceptible to sense. "If a man should speak to me [about] *immaterial substances,* or about a *free* subject, a *free will...,* I should not say that he were in error," Hobbes writes, "but that his words were without meaning; that is to say, absurd." Statements about things that never have been "nor can be incident to sense," are, according to Hobbes, "absurd speeches, taken upon credit, *without any signification at all."* By the criterion here proposed, meaningless speech is speech the terms of which do not refer to sensible or perceptible bodies; meaningful speech consists entirely of words that refer to or designate things which exist in the world of bodies. Implicit in this view is the error of supposing that to name something is to assert the real existence of that which is named, as well as a failure to distinguish between (i) a purely descriptive use of the words "meaningful" and "meaningless" (according to which all words in the dictionary of a language are meaningful and only nonsense syllables are meaningless) and (ii) a eulogistic and dyslogistic use of "meaningful" and "meaningless" which identifies the meaningful with the true and the meaningless with the false.

Leibniz conceived a plan for putting an end to all disputes in science and philosophy by doing away with ordinary speech in favor of a language which would perfectly mirror the structure of the world, and so would avoid all the misunderstandings that arise from the use of ordinary language. Leibniz's plan was grounded in the chimerical notion that the world consists ultimately of impervious and eternal simples, or primary elements, which need only to be pointed to by a sound or mark in order to be perfectly intelligible. The sounds or marks used to indicate these simple elements of reality would be true and perfect proper names. They would constitute a set of "universal characteristics" or an "alphabet of thought." Each would have an absolutely unique denotation without having any connotation whatsoever. Right reasoning would consist solely in the proper ordering of these perfect proper names according to the pattern in reality exhibited by the simples thus named or designated.

The innovations introduced by Hobbes and Leibniz come together in our own century in Bertrand Russell's theory of descriptions. The theory of descriptions is a logical device for reconstructing language in the fashion of Leibniz, except that, in place of Leibniz's ultimate simples, Russell substitutes whatever beliefs about the components and structure of reality happen to be held by the philosopher doing the reconstructing. His own ontological commitments happened to be very close to those held by Hobbes; and, in addition, he adopted from Hobbes the view that the referential significance of words consists entirely in their denotation of real existences, whatever they are. Words that lack such existential denotation are also totally without referential significance. For Russell as for Hobbes, naming is asserting; and the only words that have referential meaning are those which occupy the position of the subject term in affirmative existential propositions that are true.

The controversy surrounding Russell's theory of descriptions, the chief contributors to which were Frege, Meinong, Strawson, Quine, and Sellars, retained this focus on the existential denotation of subject terms in propositions. The combination of the innovations concerning language which were introduced by Hobbes and Leibniz made this highly restrictive focus inevitable. In ordinary speech, there is no comparable restriction that specifies which words may function as the subjects of sentences—none except, perhaps, the purely grammatical restriction that precludes particles from performing that function.

The entire program of logical analysis, which began with Russell's theory of descriptions, together with all the disputes generated by it, has no bearing at all on the problem of meaning in the broader sense which involves the difference between the meaninglessness of a nonsense syllable and the meaningfulness of every word in the dictionary of a language. The logical analysts acknowledge the difference between lexical meaning and the existential denotation of a very special set of terms, which have the character of "logically proper names." However, they do not explain this difference; they take it for granted as they engage in the reconstruction of all statements which do not conform to one or another supposed arrangement of the constituents of reality. What remains after such reconstructions are accomplished is a language in which the only words that can function with referential meaning as subjects of sentences are (i) words that have meaning in Hobbes's special sense, which is existential denotation, and (ii) words that are treated as if they were proper names in Leibniz's sense, which involves their being designative of the ultimate constituents of reality.

In consequence, the program of logical analysis does not produce a philosophy of language that is an adequate account of either ordinary or philosophical discourse. What we are given instead is a plan for restructuring the universe of discourse to make it isomorphic with the structure of reality—or, rather, with a network of beliefs about reality, all of them ontological commitments made prior to the consideration of language itself.

Within the tradition of analytic and linguistic philosophy, as developed in the twentieth century, it was Wittgenstein's *Tractatus-Logico-Philosophicus* that spelled out most clearly the ontological framework presupposed by Russell's program, following Leibniz, of making the structure of language isomorphic with the structure of reality by employing a series of logical devices. It was Wittgenstein also who was the first to realize, belatedly, the incompatibility of the ideal language game with the actual functions which language performs in daily life and in ordinary discourse. In his later work, *Philosophical Investigations*, Wittgenstein returned to a much broader conception of meaning as distinct from existential denotation. He did this by dint of a painfully detailed analysis of ordinary speech, designed to show that any reconstruction of ordinary speech in terms of existential denotation is based on a given philosopher's prior ontological commitments or belief about reality, disguised under the cloak of a logistical system. This gave rise, within the tradition of analytic and linguistic philosophy, to the movement or school which is devoted to the analysis of ordinary language or everyday speech. Although it is a move in the right direction, this approach to language shares one feature in common with the program of logical reconstruction it seeks to replace; namely, that it provides no account of meaning in the broad sense adopted by Wittgenstein, no solution of the basic problem of how meaningless notations become the meaningful words which are recorded in the lexicon of any language; and consequently, no account of how ordinary language is successfully used for the purposes of communication. In short, it fails to provide us with the essential rudiments of a sound and adequate philosophy of language.

I can sum this up by stating the three questions to be answered by a philosophy of language, and answered first and foremost because they underlie all other questions that can be raised about language. After the questions have been stated, I will then, by reference to them, characterize three approaches to the consideration of language, only the third of which I regard as sound and fruitful.

The three fundamental questions are as follows:

I. What is it that confers referential meaning on otherwise meaningless marks or sounds, thus making them into the meaningful words of a language? This is a question about the genesis of meaning.

II. What is it that meaningful words refer to when they have referential significance? This is a question about the referents of name-words, not of all words, for particles do not have referential significance.

III. What is the character of human discourse in its use of ordinary language? Can ordinary language be used satisfactorily by the philosopher as well as by others for the purpose of communication and for the expression of knowledge; or must it be replaced by a much better instrument logically devised to do what ordinary language cannot do? This is a question which asks whether ordinary language really does what it appears to be doing, or instead deceives us because it does not do what it appears to be doing.

The three different approaches to the philosophical consideration of language are as follows:

A. *The syntactical approach,* of which Russell's program of logical syntax is an example. This approach answers the third of the foregoing questions by rejecting ordinary language and by replacing it with a logically constructed or syntaxed language which reflects a series of prior ontological commitments. It, therefore, sees no need at all to answer Question I; and its answer to Question II is as follows: since referential meaning is identical with existential denotation, the referent is always a real existent.

B. *The "ordinary language" approach,* exemplified by the later Wittgenstein and his followers. This approach answers Question III to the extent that it favors the retention of ordinary language for philosophical as well as for ordinary discourse. However, it fails to explain why and how ordinary language can be used successfully for these purposes because it totally sidesteps Question I, and because its inadequate answer to Question II consists merely in the observation that some words have referential meaning and some do not, with the additional observation that it is better to treat all words as if they did not have referential meaning and so, instead of looking for their referents, pay attention to how they are used.

C. *The semantic and lexical approach,* exemplified by the philosophy of language set forth in this book. This approach also commits itself to ordinary language as a satisfactory instrument of both philosophical and everyday discourse. It answers Question III by showing that human discourse, using ordinary language, really does what it appears to be doing, and it is able to show this by the way in which it answers Questions I and II: Question I by explaining the genesis of referential meaning by the voluntary imposition of meaningless notations on the objects of our apprehension; Question II by seeing that apprehended objects are the referents of the name-words we use. And although the answers it gives to Questions I and II involve philosophical presuppositions and certain ontological and psychological posits, none of these is a prior commitment; all are posterior to the consideration of language itself.

The third approach has its roots in an earlier philosophical tradition which originated with Aristotle, was elaborated by Aquinas, and was applied to the consideration of language by Jean Poinsot, a contemporary of Thomas Hobbes. Poinsot wrote a systematic treatise on signs that dealt with the fundamental problems of meaning and laid down the basis for the answers which the third approach gives to Questions I and II. If Poinsot's influence had prevailed in modern times, instead of that of Hobbes and Leibniz, modern thought might have been spared many of the little errors which have had such serious consequences not only for philosophy in general, but for the philosophy of language in particular. In addition to Poinsot, Edmund Husserl and his followers are modern authors who approach the consideration of language without prior logical or ontological commitments and with insights that contribute to the solution of the basic questions about meaning. The rudiments of a sound and adequate approach to the philosophy of language can be found in modern thought, but not within the orbit of what, in the twentieth century, has come to be called "linguistic philosophy."

Bibliographical Appendix

As outlined in the Preface, this Bibliographical Appendix is divided into four sections, as follows:

Section I. Books and essays that advance theories or views with which the theory expounded in this book is in disagreement on fundamentals in respect to both substance and method of approach.

Section II. Books and essays that advance theories or views with which, in certain respects, the theory expounded in this book agrees, while disagreeing in other respects.

Section III. Writers who provide insights or present analyses with which the theory expounded in this book is in agreement on essentials, while diverging from them, by modification, omission, or amplification, on certain points of analysis.

Section IV. Books and essays that are of minor or peripheral relevance to the questions considered in this book.

In Sections I, II, and III the principal authors are arranged in a roughly chronological order, followed by secondary writers and commentators arranged in alphabetical order. In Section IV, the writers are listed in alphabetical order.

Section I

Thomas Hobbes: *Leviathan,* Part I, Chapters IV-V.

G. W. Leibniz: "Fundamenta Calculi Ratiocinatoris," in *Opera Philosophica quae exstant Latina Gallica Germanica Omnia,* facsimile of J. E. Erdmann's 1840 edition with additions by Renate Vollbrecht, Aalen, Germany, 1959, p. 93.

――――. "Guilielmi Pacidii Plus Ultra," in *ibid.,* p. 89.

――――. "De Scientia Universali seu Calculo Philosophico," in *ibid.,* p. 84.

――――. "Letter to Gabriel Wagner on the Value of Logic, 1696," in *Philosophical Papers and Letters,* trans. and ed. by L. E. Loemker, Chicago, 1956: Volume II, p. 756.

――――. *Selections,* ed. by Philip P. Wiener, New York, 1951: pp. 3-29; 281-290.

――――. *New Essays Concerning Human Understanding,* 3rd ed., trans. by Alfred Gideon Langley, La Salle, Ill., 1949.

George Berkeley: *The Principles of Human Knowledge,* Introduction, esp. Paragraphs 11-24.

David Hume: *Treatise of Human Nature,* Part I, Section VII; Part II, Section VI.

――――. *An Enquiry Concerning Human Understanding,* Section II; Section XII, Part II.

John Stuart Mill: *A System of Logic,* Book I, Chapters II-III.

Gottlob Frege: *The Basic Laws of Arithmetic,* trans. and ed. by Montgomery Furth, Berkeley and Los Angeles, 1964: esp. *Exposition of the System.*

――――. "Begriffsschrift (Chapter I)," trans. by P. T. Geach, in *Translations from the Philosophical Writings of Gottlob Frege,* ed. by Peter Geach and Max Black, Oxford, 1952.

――――. "Function and Concept," trans. by P. T. Geach, in *ibid.*

――――. "On Concept and Object," trans. by P. T. Geach, in *ibid.*

――――. "On Sense and Reference," trans. by Max Black, in *ibid.*

――――. "What is a Function?", trans. by P. T. Geach, in *ibid.*

————. "Negation," trans. by P. T. Geach, in *ibid.*

————. "Frege on Definitions," trans. by P. T. Geach, in *ibid.*

————. "Frege Against the Formalists," trans. by Max Black, in *ibid.*

————. "Frege on Russell's Paradox," trans. by P. T. Geach, in *ibid.*

————. "The Thought: A Logical Inquiry," trans. by A. M. and M. Quinton, in *Essays on Frege*, ed. by E. D. Klemke, Urbana, Ill., 1968.

————. "Compound Thoughts," trans. by R. H. Stoothoff, in *ibid.*

————. "On Sense and Nominatum," in *Readings in Philosophical Analysis*, ed. by Herbert Feigl and Wilfrid Sellars, New York, 1949; in *Contemporary Readings in Logical Theory*, ed. by Irving M. Copi and James A. Gould, New York, 1967.

Bertrand Russell: *A Critical Exposition of the Philosophy of Leibniz*, London, 1900: Chapter XIV.

————. *The Principles of Mathematics*, London, 1903: Chapters IV-VII; Appendices A-B.

————. "Description," in *Semantics and the Philosophy of Language: A Collection of Readings*, ed. by Leonard Linsky, Urbana, Ill., 1952.

————. "Meinong's Theory of Complexes and Assumptions," in *Mind*, N.S., Vol. XIII, 1904.

————. "Review of *Untersuchungen zur Gegendstandstheorie und Psychologie,*" by A. Meinong, Leipzig, 1904, in *Mind*, Vol. XIV, 1905.

————. "On Denoting (1905)," in *Logic and Knowledge: Essays 1901-1950*, ed. by Robert Charles Marsh, New York, 1956; in *Readings in Philosophical Analysis*, ed. by Herbert Feigl and Wilfrid Sellars, New York, 1949.

————. "Review of *Über die Stellung der Gegendstandstheorie in System der Wissenschaften,*" by A. Meinong, in *Mind*, Vol. XIV, 1907.

Bertrand Russell and Alfred North Whitehead: *Principia Mathematica*, Cambridge, 1910: Volume I, Part I, Section B, 14.

Bertrand Russell: "Knowledge by Acquaintance and Knowledge by Description," in *Proceedings of the Aristotelian Society*, N.S., Vol. XI, 1910-1911.

————. "On the Relations of Universals and Particulars (1911)," in *Logic and Knowledge: Essays 1901-1950*, ed. by Robert Charles Marsh, New York, 1956.

————. *The Problems of Philosophy*, London, 1912: Chapters IX-X.

————. "Logic as the Essence of Philosophy," in *Our Knowledge of the External World*, London, 1914.

————. "The Philosophy of Logical Atomism (1918)," in *Logic and Knowledge: Essays 1901-1950*, ed. by Robert Charles Marsh, New York, 1956.

————. *Introduction to Mathematical Philosophy*, London, 1919: Chapters 15-17.

————. "The Meaning of Meaning," in *Mind*, N.S., Vol. XXIX, 1930.

————. *The Analysis of Mind*, London and New York, 1921: Chapters X-XIII.

————. "Logical Atomism (1924)," in *Logic and Knowledge: Essays 1901-1950*, ed. by Robert Charles Marsh, New York, 1956.

————. *An Outline of Philosophy*, London, 1927: Chapter IV.

————. *An Inquiry Into Meaning and Truth*, London, 1940: esp. Chapters I-VI, XII-XV, XXI-XXV.

————. "On the Nature of Acquaintance (1941)," in *Logic and Knowledge: Essays 1901-1950*, ed. by Robert Charles Marsh, New York, 1956.

————. *Human Knowledge: Its Scope and Limits*, New York, 1948: Part II.

————. "Mr. Strawson on Referring," in *Mind*, N.S., Vol. LXVI, July, 1957; in *Classics of Analytic Philosophy*, ed. by Robert R. Ammerman, New York, 1965; in *Contemporary Readings in Logical Theory*, ed. by Irving M. Copi and James A. Gould, New York, 1967.

————. *My Philosophical Development*, New York, 1959: pp. 165-166.

L. Couturat: *La Logique de Leibniz*, Paris, 1901: p. 441.

R. F. A. Hoernlé: *Studies in Contemporary Metaphysics*, New York, 1920: Chapter IV.

————. "A Plea for a Phenomenology of Meaning," in *Proceedings of the Aristotelian Society*, N.S., Vol. XXI, 1921.

Ludwig Wittgenstein: *Tractatus Logico-Philosophicus*, London, 1922.

————. *Zettel*, ed. by G. E. M. Anscombe and G. H. von Wright, Berkeley and Los Angeles, 1967.

————. *Notebooks 1914-1916*, ed. by G. H. von Wright and G. E. M. Anscombe, Oxford, 1961.

————. *The Blue and The Brown Books*, Oxford, 1958.

————. *Philosophical Investigations*, trans. by G. E. M. Anscombe, Oxford, 1953.

C. K. Ogden and I. A. Richards: *The Meaning of Meaning*, New York, 1923.

F. C. S. Schiller: "The Meaning of 'Meaning,' " in *Mind*, N.S., Vol. XXIX, 1930.

Moritz Schlick: "Meaning and Verification," in *The Philosophical Review*, Vol. XLV, July, 1936; in *Readings in Philosophical Analysis*, ed. by Herbert Feigl and Wilfrid Sellars, New York, 1949.

Charles Morris: *Signs, Language, and Behavior*, New York, 1946: Chapters I-III; Appendix.

———. *Signification and Significance: A Study of the Relations of Signs and Values*, Cambridge, Mass., 1964: Chapter 1.

———. "Foundations of the Theory of Signs," in *Foundations of the Unity of Science*, Vol. I, No. 2, 1938.

A. J. Ayer: *Thinking and Meaning*, London, 1947.

———. "Philosophy and Language," in *Clarity Is Not Enough*, ed. by H. D. Lewis, London, 1963.

———. "Meaning and Intentionality," in *Proceedings of the XIIth International Congress of Philosophy*, Florence, Italy, 1958: p. 153. Reprinted in *Problems in the Philosophy of Language*, ed. by T. M. Olshewsky, New York, 1969: p. 241.

Gilbert Ryle: *The Concept of Mind*, New York, 1949: pp. 327-330.

———. "Ordinary Language," in *The Philosophical Review*, Vol. LXII, No. 2, April, 1953.

———. "The Theory of Meaning," in *British Philosophy in the Mid-Century: A Cambridge Symposium*, ed. by C. A. Mace, London, 1966; in *Philosophy and Ordinary Language*, ed. by Charles E. Caton, Urbana, Ill., 1963.

———. "Use, Usage and Meaning," in *The Theory of Meaning*, ed. by G. H. R. Parkinson, Oxford, 1968.

———. "Intentionality-Theory and the Nature of Thinking," in *Revue Internationale de Philosophie*, No. 104-105, 1973, Fasc. 2-3.

Charles E. Osgood: *Method and Theory in Experimental Psychology*, New York, 1953: Part IV, Chapters 15-16.

C. E. Osgood, G. Suci, and P. Tannenbaum: "The Logic of Semantic Differentiation," in *Psycholinguistics: A Book of Readings*, ed. by Sol Saporta, New York, 1961.

W. F. Sellars: "Presupposing," in *The Philosophical Review*, Vol. LXIII, April, 1954: pp. 197-215.

———. *Science, Perception, and Reality*, New York, 1963: pp. 41-59.

———. "Realism and the New Way of Words," in *Readings in Philosophical Analysis*, ed. by Herbert Feigl and Wilfrid Sellars, New York, 1949.

Niels Christensen: "A Proof that Meanings are Neither Ideas Nor Concepts," in *Analysis*, Vol. 17, October, 1956.

————. *On the Nature of Meanings: A Philosophical Analysis,* Copenhagen, 1965.

————. "On the Nature of Meanings," in *Analysis,* Vol. 16, 1965.

P. F. Strawson: *Introduction to Logical Theory,* London, 1952: Chapter 6.

————. "Identifying Reference and Truth-Values," in *Theoria,* Vol. XXX, 1964.

————. "On Referring," in *Classics of Analytic Philosophy,* ed. by Robert R. Ammerman, New York, 1965; in *Contemporary Readings in Logical Theory,* ed. by Irving M. Copi and James A. Gould, New York, 1967; in *Essays in Conceptual Analysis,* ed. by Antony Flew, London and New York, 1956; in *Philosophy and Ordinary Language,* ed. by Charles E. Caton, Urbana, Ill., 1963; in *The Theory of Meaning,* ed. by G. H. R. Parkinson, Oxford, 1968.

————. "A Reply to Mr. Sellars," in *The Philosophical Review,* Vol. LXIII, 1954.

B. F. Skinner: *Verbal Behavior,* New York, 1957.

————. "A Functional Analysis of Verbal Behavior," in *Psycholinguistics: A Book of Readings,* ed. by Sol Saporta, New York, 1961.

————. "The Problem of Reference," in *ibid.*

Carl G. Hempel: "The Empiricist Criterion of Meaning," in *Logical Positivism,* ed. by A. J. Ayer, Glencoe, Ill., 1959.

————. "Problems and Changes in the Empiricist Criterion of Meaning," in *Classics of Analytic Philosophy,* ed. by Robert R. Ammerman, New York, 1965; in *Semantics and the Philosophy of Language: A Collection of Readings,* ed. by Leonard Linsky, Urbana, Ill., 1952.

John Austin: "The Meaning of a Word," in *Philosophical Papers,* ed. by J. O. Urmson and G. J. Warnock, Oxford, 1961; in *Philosophy and Ordinary Language,* ed. by Charles E. Caton, Urbana, Ill., 1963; in *Theory of Meaning,* ed. by Adrienne and Keith Lehrer, Englewood Cliffs, N.J., 1970; in *Analyticity,* ed. by James F. Harris, Jr. and Richard H. Severens, Chicago, 1970.

W. V. Quine: *Methods of Logic,* New York, 1959: pp. 215-219, 220-224.

————. *Word and Object,* Cambridge, Mass., 1960.

————. *From A Logical Point of View,* New York, 1961: pp. 8-9, 130-138.

————. *Selected Logic Papers,* New York, 1966.

————. *Ontological Relativity and Other Essays,* New York and London, 1969.

————. *The Roots of Reference,* La Salle, Ill., 1974.

————. "The Problem of Meaning in Linguistics," in *The Structure of Language: Readings in the Philosophy of Language*, ed. by Jerry A. Fodor and Jerrold J. Katz, Englewood Cliffs, N.J., 1964; in *Psycholinguistics: A Book of Readings*, ed. by Sol Saporta, New York, 1961.

————. "Speaking of Objects," in *The Structure of Language: Readings in the Philosophy of Language*, ed. by Jerry A. Fodor and Jerrold J. Katz, Englewood Cliffs, N. J., 1964.

————. "Meaning and Translation," in *ibid*.

————. "Designation and Existence," in *Readings in Philosophical Analysis*, ed. by Herbert Feigl and Wilfrid Sellars, New York, 1949.

————. "Philosophical Progress in Language Theory," in *Metaphilosophy*, Vol. I, January, 1970: pp. 2-19.

————. "On What There Is," in *The Problem of Universals*, ed. by Charles Landesman, New York and London, 1971; in *Semantics and the Philosophy of Language*, ed. by Leonard Linsky, Chicago, 1952.

Michael Dummett: *Frege: Philosophy of Language*, New York, 1973.

————. "Nominalism," in *Essays on Frege*, ed. by E. D. Klemke, Urbana, Ill., 1968.

————. "Note: Frege on Functions," in *ibid*.

————————

William P. Alston: *"The Quest for Meanings," in Mind*, Vol. LXXII, No. 285, January, 1963.

————. "Meaning and Use," in *The Philosophical Quarterly*, Vol. 13, April, 1963; in *The Theory of Meaning*, ed. by G. H. R. Parkinson, Oxford, 1968.

————. *Philosophy of Language*, Englewood Cliffs, N.J., 1964.

————. "Meaning," in *The Encyclopedia of Philosophy*, ed. by Paul Edwards, Vol. V, New York, 1967.

————. "Theories of Meaning," in *Theory of Meaning*, ed. by Adrienne and Keith Lehrer, Englewood Cliffs, N.J., 1970.

László Antal: *Content, Meaning, and Understanding*, The Hague, 1964.

————. *Questions of Meaning*, The Hague, 1963.

Max Black: *Language and Philosophy: Studies in Method*, Ithaca, N.Y., 1949: Chapters V-VIII.

————. "Language and Reality," in *Proceedings and Addresses of the American Philosophical Association*, Vol. XXXII, October, 1959; in

Clarity Is Not Enough, ed. by H. D. Lewis, London, 1963; in *The Linguistic Turn: Recent Essays in Philosophical Method,* ed. by Richard Rorty, Chicago and London, 1967.

———. *Models and Metaphors: Studies in Language and Philosophy,* Ithaca, N. Y., 1962: Chapters I-II, VI-VII.

Roger W. Brown: *Words and Things: An Introduction to Language,* New York and London, 1958: Chapter III.

Roger W. Brown and Don E. Dulaney: "A Stimulus-Response Analysis of Language and Meaning," in *Language, Thought, and Culture,* ed. by Paul Henle, Ann Arbor, Mich., 1965.

L. J. Cohen: *The Diversity of Meaning,* New York, 1963.

James W. Cornman: "Language and Ontology," in *The Linguistic Turn: Recent Essays in Philosophical Method,* ed. by Richard Rorty, Chicago and London, 1967.

———. *Metaphysics, Reference, and Language,* New Haven and London, 1966.

———. "Uses of Language and Philosophical Problems," in *The Linguistic Turn: Recent Essays in Philosophical Method,* ed. by Richard Rorty, Chicago and London, 1967.

Ralph Monroe Eaton: *Symbolism and Truth: An Introduction to the Theory of Knowledge,* New York, 1964.

William K. Frankena: "Some Aspects of Language," in *Language, Thought, and Culture,* ed. by Paul Henle, Ann Arbor, Mich., 1965.

Nelson Goodman: "On Likeness of Meaning," in *Semantics and the Philosophy of Language,* ed. by Leonard Linsky, Urbana, Ill., 1952; in *Philosophy and Analysis,* ed. by Margaret Macdonald, New York, 1954.

———. "On Some Differences About Meaning," in *Philosophy and Analysis,* ed. by Margaret Macdonald, New York, 1954.

H. P. Grice: "Meaning," in *The Philosophical Review,* Vol. LXVI, July, 1957.

Charles Landesman: *Discourse and Its Presuppositions,* New Haven and London, 1972.

Adrienne Lehrer: "Meaning in Linguistics," in *Theory of Meaning,* ed. by Adrienne and Keith Lehrer, Englewood Cliffs, N.J., 1970.

Keith Lehrer: "Meaning in Philosophy," in *ibid.*

Leonard Linsky: "Reference and Referents," in *Philosophy and Ordinary Language,* ed. by Charles E. Caton, Urbana, Ill., 1963.

————. *Referring*, London and New York, 1967.

A. M. MacIver: "Demonstratives and Proper Names," in *Philosophy and Analysis*, ed. by Margaret Macdonald, New York, 1954.

Graham Nerlich: "A Scrutiny of Reference," in *Canadian Journal of Philosophy*, Vol. I, No. 3, 1972.

John R. Searle: *Speech Acts: An Essay in the Philosophy of Language*, Cambridge, 1969.

————. "Meaning and Speech Acts," in *The Philosophical Review*, Vol. LXXI, October, 1962; in *Theory of Meaning*, ed. by Adrienne and Keith Lehrer, Englewood Cliffs, N.J., 1970.

————. "Proper Names," in *Philosophy and Ordinary Language*, ed. by Charles E. Caton, Urbana, Ill., 1963.

Rulon Wells: "Meaning and Use," in *Psycholinguistics: A Book of Readings*, ed. by Sol Saporta, New York, 1961; in *Theory of Meaning*, ed. by Adrienne and Keith Lehrer, Englewood Cliffs, N. J., 1970.

Paul Ziff: "On H. P. Grice's Account of Meaning," in *Analysis*, Vol. 28, October, 1967.

————————

G. E. M. Anscombe: *An Introduction to Wittgenstein's Tractatus*, New York, 1965: Chapters 2, 6-7.

A. J. Ayer: *Russell and Moore: The Analytical Heritage*, Cambridge, Mass., 1971: Chapter 2.

Gustav Bergmann: "Ontological Alternatives," in *Essays on Frege*, ed. by E. D. Klemke, Urbana, Ill., 1968.

————. "Frege's Hidden Nominalism," in *ibid*.

James Bartlett: "On Questioning the Validity of Frege's Concept of Function," in *ibid*.

Max Black: "Frege on Functions," in *ibid*.

Charles E. Caton: "An Apparent Difficulty in Frege's Ontology," in *ibid*.

Robert J. Clack: *Bertrand Russell's Philosophy of Language*, The Hague, 1969.

John W. Cook: "Solipsism and Language," in *Ludwig Wittgenstein: Philosophy and Language*, ed. by Alice Ambrose and Morris Lazerowitz, London and New York, 1972.

E. Daitz: "The Picture Theory of Meaning," in *Essays in Conceptual Analysis*, ed. by Antony Flew, London and New York, 1956.

Frank Ebersole: "Saying and Meaning," in *Ludwig Wittgenstein: Philosophy and Language*, ed. by Alice Ambrose and Morris Lazerowitz, London and New York, 1972.

E. J. Furlong: "Berkeley's Theory of Meaning," in *Mind*, Vol. LXXIII, July, 1964.

Richard Gale: "Strawson's Restricted Theory of Referring," in *The Philosophical Quarterly*, Vol. XX, 1970.

P. T. Geach: "Russell's Theory of Descriptions," in *Philosophy and Analysis*, ed. by Margaret Macdonald, New York, 1954.

———. "Frege," in *Three Philosophers*, Oxford, 1963.

———. "Naming and Predicating," in *Essays on Frege*, ed. by E. D. Klemke, Urbana, Ill., 1968.

———. "Class and Concept," in *ibid*.

M. S. Gram: "Frege, Concepts, and Ontology," in *ibid*.

Reinhardt Grossmann: "Frege's Ontology," in *ibid*.

Garth Hallett: *Wittgenstein's Definition of Meaning as Use*, New York, 1967.

Gilbert Harman: "Quine on Meaning and Existence," in *The Review of Metaphysics*, Vol. XXI, December, 1967.

H. Hochberg: "Strawson, Russell, and the King of France," in *Philosophy of Science*, Vol. XXXVII, 1970.

Howard Jackson: "Frege's Ontology," in *Essays on Frege*, ed. by E. D. Klemke, Urbana, Ill., 1968.

W. E. Kennick: "Philosophy as Grammar and the Reality of Universals," in *Ludwig Wittgenstein: Philosophy and Language*, ed. by Alice Ambrose and Morris Lazerowitz, London and New York, 1972.

E. D. Klemke: "Frege's Ontology: Realism," in *Essays on Frege*, ed. by E. D. Klemke, Urbana, Ill., 1968.

———. "Professor Bergmann and Frege's 'Hidden Nominalism,' " in *ibid*.

F. J. Leavitt: "On Strawson's Revised Position on Identifying Reference," in *Theoria*, Vol. XXXV, 1969.

William Marshall: "Frege's Theory of Functions and Objects," in *Essays on Frege*, ed. by E. D. Klemke, Urbana, Ill., 1968.

———. "Sense and Reference: A Reply," in *ibid*.

G. E. Moore: "Russell's 'Theory of Descriptions,' " in *Philosophical Papers*, New York, 1962.

———. "Wittgenstein's Lectures in 1930-1933," in *Classics of Analytic Philosophy*, ed. by Robert R. Ammerman, New York, 1965.

James C. Morrison: *Meaning and Truth in Wittgenstein's Tractatus*, The Hague, 1968.

George Pitcher: *The Philosophy of Wittgenstein*, Englewood Cliffs, N. J., 1964: Part II, esp. Chapters 10-12.

John R. Searle: "Russell's Objections to Frege's Theory of Sense and Reference," in *Essays on Frege*, ed. by E. D. Klemke, Urbana, Ill., 1968.

Robert Sternfeld: *Frege's Logical Theory*, Carbondale, Ill., 1966.

Jeremy D. B. Walker: *A Study of Frege*, Ithaca, N. Y., 1965.

Rulon Wells: "Frege's Ontology," in *Essays on Frege*, ed. by E. D. Klemke, Urbana, Ill., 1968.

———. "Is Frege's Concept of a Function Valid?", in *ibid.*

Paul D. Wienpahl: "Frege's Sinn und Bedeutung," in *ibid.*

John Wisdom: "Wittgenstein on 'Private Language,'" in *Ludwig Wittgenstein: Philosophy and Language*, ed. by Alice Ambrose and Morris Lazerowitz, London and New York, 1972.

Section II

John Locke: *An Essay Concerning Human Understanding*, Book III.

F. H. Bradley: *The Principles of Logic*, London, 1883: Book I, Chapter 1, pp. 2-8.

Franz Brentano: *The True and the Evident*, trans. by Roderick M. Chisholm, Ilse Politzer, and Kurt R. Fischer, New York, 1966: Part Two, Chapter III: Part Three, Chapters I-II; Appendices, Chapter II.

———. "Genuine and Fictitious Objects," trans. by D. B. Terrell, in *Realism and the Background of Phenomenology*, ed. by Roderick M. Chisholm, Glencoe, Ill., 1960.

———. "The Distinction Between Mental and Physical Phenomena," in *ibid.*

———. "Presentation and Judgment Form Two Distinct Fundamental Classes," in *ibid.*

R. F. A. Hoernlé: "Image, Idea and Meaning," in *Mind* N. S., Vol. XVI, 1907.

H. H. Joachim: "The Meaning of 'Meaning,'" in *Mind*, N.S., Vol. XXIX, 1930.

Clarence Irving Lewis: "Experience and Meaning," in *Collected Papers of Clarence Irving Lewis*, ed. by John D. Goheen and John L. Mothershead, Jr., Stanford, Calif., 1970.

———. "The Modes of Meaning," in *ibid.*

Brand Blanshard: *The Nature of Thought*, London, 1939: Book Two, Chapters VIII-IX.

H. H. Price: *Thinking and Experience*, London, 1953: esp. pp. 160-233, 288-296, 327-357.

————. "Thinking and Representation," in *Proceedings of the British Academy*, 1947.

Paul Henle: "The Problem of Meaning," in *Proceedings of the American Philosophical Society*, Vol. XXVII, 1954.

————. "Do We Discover Our Uses of Words?", in *The Linguistic Turn: Recent Essays in Philosophical Method*, ed. by Richard Rorty, Chicago, 1967.

Morris Lazerowitz: *The Structure of Metaphysics*, London, 1955: Chapters III, XI.

F. Waismann: *The Principles of Linguistic Philosophy*, ed. by R. Harré, New York, 1965: Part II, Chapters VI, VIII, X-XII, XVI.

Karl R. Popper: *Objective Knowledge: An Evolutionary Approach*, Oxford, 1972: Chapter 4.

Roderick M. Chisholm: "Brentano on Descriptive Psychology and the Intentional," in *Introduction to the Philosophy of Mind*, ed. by Harold Morick, New York, 1970; in *Phenomenology and Existentialism*, ed. by Edward N. Lee and Maurice Mandelbaum, Baltimore, Md., 1967.

————. "Intentionality and the Mental," in Minnesota Studies in the Philosophy of Science, Volume II: *Concepts, Theories, and the Mind-Body Problem*, ed. by Herbert Feigl, Michael Scriven, and Grover Maxwell, Minneapolis, 1958.

————. "On Some Psychological Concepts and the 'Logic' of Intentionality," with Comments by Robert C. Sleigh, Jr., and a Rejoinder by Roderick M. Chisholm, in *Intentionality, Minds, and Perception: A Discussion on Contemporary Philosophy*, compiled by Hector-Neri Castañeda, Detroit, 1966.

Noam Chomsky: "A Review of B. F. Skinner's *Verbal Behavior*," in *The Structure of Language: Readings in the Philosophy of Language*, ed. by Jerry A. Fodor and Jerrold J. Katz, Englewood Cliffs, N.J., 1964.

P. T. Geach: *Reference and Generality: An Examination of Some Medieval and Modern Theories*, Ithaca, N.Y., 1962.

Reinhardt Grossman: "Non-Existent Objects: A Recent Work on Brentano and Meinong," in *American Philosophical Quarterly*, Vol. 6, 1969.

Section III

Aristotle: *On Interpretation*, 1, 16a 4-8.

Aristotle: *On Interpretation, Commentary by St. Thomas and Cajetan*, trans. by Jean Oesterle, Milwaukee, 1962: Lessons II-IV.

Augustine: *Concerning the Teacher*: Chapters I-VII.

———. *On Christian Doctrine*, Book I, Chapter 2; Book II, Chapters 1-4.

Aquinas: *Summa Theologica*, Part I, 13, 1; 29, 2; 34, 1; 79, 10, ad 3; 84, 7; 85, 2, ad 3; 85, 5; Part I-II, 7, 1.

John of St. Thomas [Jean Poinsot]: *Cursus philosophicus*, ed. by B. Reiser, Turin, Italy, 1930: Volume I, Part II, Qq. XXI-XXXIII, 646 a 14-749 b 47. See also Q. II, Arts. 1, 2, 4; Q. XVII, Arts. 1, 2, 3.

Alexius Meinong: *Ueber Annahmen*, Leipzig, 1910.

———. "The Theory of Objects," trans. by Isaac Levi, D. B. Terrell, and Roderick M. Chisholm, in *Realism and the Background of Phenomenology*, ed. by Roderick M. Chisholm, Glencoe, Ill., 1960.

Edmund Husserl: *Recherches Logiques*, trans. from German by Hubert Élie, in collaboration with Lothar Kelkel and René Schérer, Paris, 1961: Tome Second, Première Partie, I, Chapitre I-IV; Tome Second, Deuxième Partie, III, Chapitre I; IV.

Jacques Maritain: *Reflexions Sur L'Intelligence*, Paris, 1924: Chapters I-II.

———. *Les Degrés du Savoir*, Paris, 1932: Annexe I.

———. *The Degrees of Knowledge*, New York, 1938: Chapter III, esp. pp. 144-164.

———. *An Introduction to Logic*, New York, 1937: Chapter I, Sections 1-3.

———. *Ransoming the Time*, New York, 1941: Chapter IX, "Sign and Symbol."

———. "Language and the Theory of Sign," in *Language: An Enquiry into Its Meaning and Function*, ed. by Ruth Nanda Anshen, New York, 1957.

Yves Simon: "To Be and To Know," in *Chicago Review*, Vol. 14, No. 4, Spring, 1961.

———. *Introduction à l'ontologie du connâitre*, Paris, 1934, and Dubuque, Ia., 1965.

———. *The Great Dialogue of Nature and Space*, ed. by Gerard J. Dalcourt, Albany, N.Y., 1972: pp. 95-110.

John A. Oesterle: "The Problem of Meaning," in *The Thomist*, Vol. VI, July, 1943.

————. "Another Approach to the Problem of Meaning," in *The Thomist*, Vol. VII, April, 1944.

Bernard Lonergan: *Verbum: Word and Idea in Aquinas*, ed. by David B. Burrell, South Bend, Ind., 1967.

Etienne Gilson: *Linguistique et Philosophie*, Paris, 1969: Chapters II-IV.

John N. Deely: "The Two Approaches to Language," in *The Thomist*, Vol. XXXVIII, 1974.

————————

Gustav Bergmann: *Realism: A Critique of Brentano and Meinong*, Madison, Wisc., 1967.

Roderick M. Chisholm: "Meinong, Alexius," in *The Encyclopedia of Philosophy*, ed. by Paul Edwards, Volume 5, New York, 1967.

————. "Homeless Objects," in *Revue Internationale de Philosophie*, No. 104-105, 1973, Fasc. 2-3.

Jacques Derrida: *Speech and Phenomena and Other Essays on Husserl's Theory of Signs*, trans. by David B. Allison, Evanston, Ill., 1973.

J. N. Findlay: *Meinong's Theory of Objects and Values*, Oxford, 1963.

————. "Meinong the Phenomenologist," in *Revue Internationale de Philosophie*, No. 104-105, 1973, Fasc. 2-3.

————. "Use, Usage and Meaning," in *Clarity Is Not Enough*, ed. by H. D. Lewis, London, 1963; in *The Theory of Meaning*, ed. by G. H. R. Parkinson, Oxford, 1968.

Aron Gurwitsch: "Husserl's Theory of the Intentionality of Consciousness in Historical Perspective," in *Phenomenology and Existentialism*, ed. by Edward N. Lee and Maurice Mandelbaum, Baltimore, Md., 1967.

André Hayen: *L'intentionnel selon Saint Thomas*, Second Edition, Paris, 1954.

J. N. Mohanty: *Edmund Husserl's Theory of Meaning*, The Hague, 1969.

————. *The Concept of Intentionality*, St. Louis, Mo., 1972.

Herman Parret: "Husserl and the Neo-Humboldtians on Language," in *International Philosophical Quarterly*, Vol. XII, No. 1, March, 1972.

Paul Ricoeur: "Husserl and Wittgenstein on Language," in *Phenomenology and Existentialism*, ed. by Edward N. Lee and Maurice Mandelbaum, Baltimore, Md., 1967.

Robert Sokolowski: *The Formation of Husserl's Concept of Constitution*, The Hague, 1964: Chapter II.

Henry Veatch: *Intentional Logic*, New Haven, 1952.

Section IV

George P. Adams: "The Habitat of Meaning," in *Meaning and Interpretation*, Berkeley, 1950.

John Austin: *How to Do Things with Words*, ed. by J. O. Urmson, New York, 1962.

L. Bloomfield: "Meaning," in *Psycholinguistics: A Book of Readings*, ed. by Sol Saporta, New York, 1961.

Rudolf Carnap: *The Logical Syntax of Language*, trans. by Amethe Smeaton, London, 1937.

————. *Introduction to Semantics*, Cambridge, Mass., 1942.

————. *Meaning and Necessity: A Study in Semantics and Modal Logic*, Chicago, 1956.

————. *The Logical Structure of the World and Pseudoproblems in Philosophy*, trans. by Rolf A. George, Berkeley and Los Angeles, 1967.

————. "Testability and Meaning," in *Classics of Analytic Philosophy*, ed. by Robert R. Ammerman, New York, 1965.

W. L. Chafe: *Meaning and the Structure of Language*, Chicago, 1970.

Noam Chomsky: "Syntax and Semantics," in *Psycholinguistics: A Book of Readings*, ed. by Sol Saporta, New York, 1961.

————. *Current Issues in Linguistic Theory*, The Hague, 1964.

————. *Syntactic Structures*, The Hague, 1965.

————. *Aspects of the Theory of Syntax*, Cambridge, Mass., 1965.

————. *Cartesian Linguistics: A Chapter in the History of Rationalist Thought*, New York and London, 1966.

————. *Language and Mind*, New York, 1968.

Marcia L. Colish: *The Mirror of Language: A Study in the Medieval Theory of Knowledge*, New Haven and London, 1968.

Irving M. Copi: "The Growth of Concepts," in *Language, Thought, and Culture*, ed. by Paul Henle, Ann Arbor, Mich., 1965.

————. "Reply to Bergmann," in *The Linguistic Turn: Recent Essays in Philosophical Method*, ed. by Richard Rorty, Chicago and London, 1967.

S. Morris Engel: *Language and Illumination: Studies in the History of Philosophy*, The Hague, 1969: Chapters 1-2.

Edward Erwin: *The Concept of Meaninglessness*, Baltimore and London, 1970.

Raymond J. Firth: "Modes of Meaning," in *Papers in Linguistics: 1934-1951*, London, 1957.

Antony Flew: "Philosophy and Language," in *Essays in Conceptual Analysis*, ed. by Antony Flew, London and New York, 1956.

Charles C. Fries: "Meaning and Linguistic Analysis," in *Theory of Meaning*, ed. by Adrienne and Keith Lehrer, Englewood Cliffs, N.J., 1970.

Eugene T. Gendlin: *Experiencing and the Creation of Meaning: A Philosophical and Psychological Approach to the Subjective*, Glencoe, Ill., 1962.

Stuart Hampshire: "The Interpretation of Language: Words and Concepts," in *British Philosophy in the Mid-Century: A Cambridge Symposium*, ed. by C. A. Mace, London, 1966; in *The Linguistic Turn: Recent Essays in Philosophical Method*, ed. by Richard Rorty, Chicago and London, 1967.

――――. "Are All Philosophical Questions Questions of Language?", in *The Linguistic Turn: Recent Essays in Philosophical Method*, ed. by Richard Rorty, Chicago and London, 1967.

Bernard Harrison: *Meaning and Structure: An Essay in the Philosophy of Language*, New York, 1972.

David Holdcroft: "Meaning and Illocutionary Acts," in *The Theory of Meaning*, ed. by G. H. R. Parkinson, London, 1968.

Jerrold J. Katz: *The Philosophy of Language*, New York, 1966.

Remy C. Kwant: *Phenomenology of Language*, Pittsburgh, Pa., 1965.

John Lyons: *Noam Chomsky*, New York, 1970.

C. A. Mace: "Some Trends in the Philosophy of Mind," in *British Philosophy in the Mid-Century: A Cambridge Symposium*, ed. by C. A. Mace, London, 1966.

Paul Marhenke: "The Criterion of Significance," in *Semantics and the Philosophy of Language*, ed. by Leonard Linsky, Urbana, Ill., 1952.

Benson Mates: "Synonymity," in *Analyticity*, ed. by James F. Harris, Jr. and Richard H. Severens, Chicago, 1970.

George A. Miller: *Language and Communication*, New York, 1951.

Charles E. Osgood, George J. Suci, and Percy H. Tannenbaum: *The Measurement of Meaning*, Urbana, Ill., 1957.

Stephen R. Schiffer: *Meaning*, Oxford, 1972.

Dudley Shapere: "Philosophy and the Analysis of Language," in *The Linguistic Turn: Recent Essays in Philosophical Method*, ed. by Richard Rorty, Chicago and London, 1967.

Daniel M. Taylor: *Explanation and Meaning: An Introduction to Philosophy*, London and New York, 1970.

Robert F. Terwilliger: *Meaning and Mind: A Study in the Psychology of Language*, New York, 1968.

William Todd: "Intentionality and the Theory of Meaning," in *Philosophical Studies*, Vol. XVII, June, 1964.

Stephen Ullmann: *The Principles of Semantics*, New York, 1951.

Wilbur Marshall Urban: *Language and Reality: The Philosophy of Language and the Principles of Symbolism*, London and New York, 1939.

V. Welby: *What Is Meaning?: Studies in the Development of Significance*, London, 1903.

Paul Ziff: *Semantic Analysis*, Ithaca, N.Y., 1960.

————. *Understanding Understanding*, Ithaca and London, 1972.